FACILITY MANAGEMENT FOR CHURCHES

MAINTAINING THE HOUSE OF WORSHIP IN EASY-TO-UNDERSTAND CONCEPTS

JAMES D. JORDAN

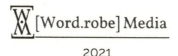

[Word.robe] Media

2021

FACILITY MANAGEMENT FOR CHURCHES:
Maintaining the House of Worship in Easy-To-Understand Concepts

Copyright © 2021 by James D. Jordan

All rights reserved. No part of this book may be reproduced or transmitted in any form or by any means, electronic or mechanical, including photocopying and recording, or by any information storage and retrieval system, without permission in writing from the author.

Scripture quotations are taken from the Holy Bible:

English Standard Version, ESV ® Text Edition ® (2016), copyright © 2001 by Crossway Bibles, a publishing ministry of Good News Publishers.

New International Version ®, NIV®. Copyright © 1973, 1978, 1984, 2011 by Biblica, Inc.®

New Living Translation, NLT. Copyright © 1996, 2004, 2007, 2013, 2015 by Tyndale House Foundation, Tyndale House Publishers, Inc.

First Edition, March 2021

ISBN-9798573501888

Published by Wordrobe Media
Printed and distributed through Kindle Direct Publishing

Cover design by Jonathan Jordan
Editing and layout by Jonathan Jordan | Wordrobe Media

www.wordrobemedia.com

Dedication

Susan, you have been such an amazing soulmate for me for the last thirty-seven years. You have often had to stay home from church with sick kids and then also waited at home while I was at work at all hours, and yet you have been the most amazing and encouraging person to me as we have served our Lord together. I love you so much. You are my rock.

CONTENTS

ACKNOWLEDGEMENTS	i
FOREWORD written by Josh Patterson	iii
INTRODUCTION	1
CHAPTER 1 | Called and Empowered	5
CHAPTER 2 | A Safe Harbor	9
CHAPTER 3 | Get to Know Your Buildings:	15
The Good, The Bad, and The Ugly	
CHAPTER 4 | Setting Up Schedules:	21
So You Don't Lose Your Mind (or Your Job)	
CHAPTER 5 | Contractors and Vendors	35
CHAPTER 6 | Volunteers:	45
Manna From Heaven!	
CHAPTER 7 | The House of the Lord:	49
Do You Know All The Parts of Your Building?	
7.1 Introduction to Building Systems	49
7.2 HVAC	65
7.3 Electrical	77
7.4 Plumbing	84
7.5 Lawn Sprinklers & Property Drainage	92

7.6 Roofing	96
7.7 Security / Fire Alarm / Fire Suppression Systems	101
7.8 Exterior Safety / Parking Lots / Landscaping	105
7.9 Construction Basics	109

CHAPTER 8 | Lists, Lists, and More Lists — 129

CHAPTER 9 | Project Management: — 137
So You Really Want To Move That Wall, Huh?

CHAPTER 10 | Your Ministry Staff & Facility Staff: — 153
Working With & Loving Them

CHAPTER 11 | Tools That Every Facility Manager Needs: — 165
Yes, Real Tools!

CHAPTER 12 | Technology — 171

CHAPTER 13 | Safety Precautions — 177

CHAPTER 14 | Budgets That Make Sense and Get Things Done — 199

CHAPTER 15 | Network With Other Facility Managers — 211

CHAPTER 16 | Now Let's Start Managing Your Facilities — 215

REFERENCE SECTION — 223

ABOUT THE AUTHOR — 225

ACKNOWLEDGEMENTS

First, I want to thank my Jesus who saved me, called me, and empowers me in every part of my life. To Him alone belongs the glory.

I want to thank all the pastors I served with that recognized that I had a talent and love for overseeing the facilities and allowed me to serve in that area as well as my other ministry responsibilities. They gave me the privilege of working on building projects and overseeing maintenance needs over the last four decades. This gave me the experience I needed to become a church facility manager in God's due time.

This book is being written only because Craig Northcutt, Doug Stanley, and Lee Lewis gave me the opportunity to be a church facility manager. Craig has taught me so much about facilities management. He was always there to help me learn the job, give guidance, yet was never anything but supportive and encouraging. For this I will always be grateful.

I also want to thank my good friends and fellow facility managers Glenn Campbell and Robert Lusk, who have forgotten more about facility management than I will ever know. Glenn always encouraged me and shared facility principles and ideas with me, and Robert is the hardest working person I know. Both these men are wonderful examples of true servant leaders in Christ.

To my associate and dear brother Gary Wilson: you are a faithful, daily blessing and reminder of God's goodness. You are the best.

Also, I could never have gotten this book to print without Susan's amazing proofreading and our son Jonathan's editing and publishing skills.

FOREWORD
Written by Josh Patterson
Lead Pastor, The Village Church (Flower Mound, TX)

I've always been drawn to greatness, to giants. When I reflect on the heroes in my life, whether in film or novels, biographies, or through the pages of Scripture, I find a consistent theme: my heart is drawn toward great leaders.

Digging deeper into this theme, I've tried to understand what makes a leader great. Is it their competence and character? Is it courage and valor? In some sense, it is a combination of all of these. But, there is a common thread throughout it all: humble service.

The leaders I have been drawn to in admiration all of my life demonstrate with their life and action that there is a greater mission, a higher call, and a work that goes beyond themselves. And, in light of this recognition, they rise to greatness.

I see it in the countless heroes of WWII and the giants of the Civil Rights movement. I also see it in the quiet leadership of faithful saints who labor in prayer and those who help stack chairs in the church sanctuary. I've learned that being a giant has less to do with stature and more to do with posture; a posture of service.

James Jordan and I worked together for six years. He served as the Facilities Manager for one of our church campuses, and I served as Lead Pastor. You don't have to be around James for long to know that he is a servant, but you may not know the myriad of ways he serves. He has served all of us by giving four years of his life to the honorable work of the U.S. Air Force. He has served the church for thirty years through music ministry. He served the church for another six years through facility management until he retired. He has served me personally through consistent prayer and encouragement. And, he is serving you by writing this book. James is one of those giants.

If you are involved in church facilities through vocation or volunteerism, or if you have a desire to better understand the importance and practicalities of the work, then this book is for you. It is written in a winsome manner and puts the cookies on the shelf so that even someone like me can reach them! Reading through the book only deepened my gratitude for James and others like him.

You are likely picking up this book because you are one of those people! You desire to keep and consider the facilities the Lord has entrusted to your church. This is no small thing. You have a thousand things to juggle and often your work goes unnoticed until there is an issue – the HVAC isn't working, there is a problem in the restroom, the contractor didn't show up, and the list continues. You'll not only find a camaraderie in this book…you'll find the advice of a sage!

I want to end this foreword with a word of thanks. James, thank you for your service and the various ways you serve. This book was a keen reminder to me of the privilege I've had working alongside a great facilities team. Thank you. It doesn't happen without you. And, you, dear reader, thank you for your desire to know and grow in and around the area of church facility management. I pray you are rightly honored for the vital work you do.

INTRODUCTION

In 1967, my dear, wonderful parents decided that a ten-year-old boy with dyslexia (although undiagnosed at that time) should take piano lessons. My dad had played piano since he was nine or ten, so I guess he thought I should learn as well, and my mother, bless her heart, probably thought it would give me focus. The only problem was that Daddy had told stories how his piano teacher would hit his hands with a ruler every time he made a mistake. Now paint that picture in your mind as a ten-year-old.

So, here we go to piano lessons the first day. We pull up to this huge Victorian monstrosity of a house that, again, for a ten-year-old boy looks like it's about 400 years old and should be in Transylvania or next door to Herman Munster's house. We walk in the front door of this house and it's dark and the ceilings are high, and it's decorated like *Ripley's Believe It or Not* with ancient artifacts everywhere.

Daddy tells me the piano teacher said to just sit on the bench in the entryway until she comes for me. I sit down, HE LEAVES (I still can't believe he left me there), and I look up to see this life-size bust of some old, dead musician looking at me.

Finally, some little kid walks, or, should I say, practically runs, out of her living room, and my piano teacher, Mrs. Ragnhild Congdon, comes out and says in very proper English, "You must be James. Well, come in and let's get started."

She has me sit down at this giant pile of papers that has

piano keys sticking out of it. Only years later did I realize it was a grand piano that she had piled music on top of and next to for the last seventy-five years. Oh yes, I figured she was at least 150 years old, but she was very nice. We talked for a while and then we had a short lesson that first day.

Anyway, for the next year or more we trudged through piano lessons, finally nailing down the hymn "On Jordan's Stormy Banks," which seemed very appropriate considering how I played, or didn't play, the piano. That was the only song I remember learning.

Then one day in 1968, out of the blue, Mrs. Congdon had me sing a song as she played along. I think she did this in desperation, thinking that if I could sing the song, that maybe I could somehow come closer to playing it. When I had sung a few measures, I thought maybe she had died while playing the piano.

She just stared at me and finally said, "James, you have a beautiful voice!"

Well, that was liberation day! Hallelujah, praise the Lord! From then on, my piano lessons became voice lessons, and it was a glorious time each week. Mrs. Congdon had me try out for the Kenosha, Wisconsin Boys Choir, which I made. This life lesson taught me about finding purpose in life when you can't see it. See, Mrs. Congdon and I stumbled on to what I did well and then she helped me pursue it. I had no idea that when my piano teacher discovered that I could sing, that years later God would call me to the music ministry for nearly thirty years.

You may be wondering why I just told this story, but that's how almost every facility manager I know, including myself, got into the facility ministry. No, they didn't fail at piano less-

INTRODUCTION

ons like I did. I'll guarantee you that most facility managers never planned at twenty years old to be a church facility manager.

Most of us were involved in other ministries or had other jobs and just kind of stumbled into facilities. We were asked to help set up a room for an event, carried trash out between services, helped with a project at the church, or met a contractor to explain a repair that needed to be done. Then, one day a pastor or church leader asked if we would like to work for the church to keep the facilities up. We found a ministry where we didn't have to be in front of people, or speak publicly, or perform in front of church, but instead could use our servant's heart, our hands, and our mechanical talents to do things to help people and serve the Lord in a way that touches lives and gives personal peace and fulfillment.

If you are reading this today, I assume God has called you to the wonderful ministry of facilities as a facility manager, associate, volunteer, or properties team leader. The chapters that follow will hopefully steer you through the process of becoming the church facility manager God wants you to be. Whether your church uses a facility manager, a building and grounds committee, a facility team, or a team of volunteers to oversee the properties of the church, I hope this book will help.

There will be a lot of "nuts and bolts" talked about in the pages to follow. You may only want to use this book as a resource book, just picking and choosing which chapters to read based on your need at the time. You won't read a lot of long-worded complicated terminology in this book. You'll hear me explain in plain language the way I see things in my way of talking, which is plain and simple. Also, you may not agree with everything in this book. That's okay. Please remember this book is not a technical manual. It is written from my heart and mind and is a personal testimony of the grace of God, and how I view facility management and the facility ministry of the local church.

Whichever way you use this book, my sole desire is that God is glorified through its words. God bless you as you read and become the empowered facility manager that our Lord wants you to be. Get ready to see how the Lord can use you to touch lives every day in extraordinary ways. I hope you see facility management as an amazing opportunity to love God and love people.

CHAPTER 1
Called and Empowered

The year is somewhere around 1500 BC. There is this man who, until a few weeks ago, was a major player in the construction industry in Egypt. He could build anything and also possessed the leadership skills to oversee thousands of craftsmen and builders on projects. Pharaoh himself often used him for renovations to the palace or many of the sacred sites. He was even asked to teach other builders the newest construction methods.

The last few weeks have been very different for him. Even though he was a gifted builder, he was a slave whose family had been forced to be builders for the last 400 years. His name is Bezalel. He saw the devastation that was brought to Egypt by the plagues which had ravaged the country by the hand of God. What an amazing thing to witness!

Things happened so quickly when Pharaoh allowed the people of Israel to leave Egypt. Bezalel packed only his family's necessary belongings, leaving many of his valuable tools behind. He led his family out of Egypt alongside millions of other people. Then, just a few days after leaving Egypt on the shores of the Red Sea, he was sure he and his family would be killed by the Egyptian army, only to see, once again, the hand of God deliver them safely through the waters to the other side on dry land.

God, who for 400 years had been so silent, now seemed to be putting on a grand show at every turn. Bezalel witnessed the water coming from a rock. He then daily saw Jehovah provide food in the morning and evening.

That is where we are today. Bezalel is wondering what he can do now. He helps his wife keep the kids corralled and gathers food and sets up their tent when the mass of people stops to rest. He also occasionally helps people repair their tents. Not really the grand life for a contractor who just weeks earlier was overseeing vast projects for the world's mightiest kingdom.

Today is different, though. There's a rumor that Aaron, the brother of Moses, is looking for him. What could this be about? What could he have done? He has some friends who are not happy with the living conditions out here, but he has tried to keep to himself and take care of his loved ones and steer clear of any trouble with Moses or Aaron. Finally, he hears a crowd coming toward his tent. He steps out to see Aaron coming with what looks like a mob behind him.

Bezalel swallows nervously, then welcomes Aaron to his home. Aaron gets right to the point: Moses would like to speak to him immediately. Some of Bezalel's snarky friends who have wandered over mock him by saying, "You've done it now. Just wait until Moses gets done with you."

This just feels different, though. For some reason, there is a peace about Aaron's request. He kisses his wife and walks with Aaron the mile or so through the massive tent city to Moses's tent. Nothing is said, almost as if there is a sacredness to what is going on. He can't help wondering a little if Moses needs something done to his tent, yet this feels bigger than that.

As they approach the tent of the Hebrew leader, Moses steps out and stretches his arms wide as if to embrace

CHAPTER 1: CALLED AND EMPOWERED

Bezalel. Everyone knows that hugging Moses is not done, especially since he came down from Mount Sinai with the tablets from the Lord with his face glowing like a giant firefly.

Bezalel stops and kneels.

Moses then asks Bezalel to get up and join him in his tent. "Bezalel, I have news for you," Moses says in a very serious tone. "God has chosen you. God has given me the plans to build Him a dwelling place and has said you, Bezalel, son of Uri, will be responsible for getting the project completed."

At that very moment, something happens to him. He feels like himself physically, yet he feels empowered by something beyond him.

Moses then tells him, "Bezalel, the Spirit of God has come upon you and given you the ability to oversee the building of the tabernacle."

From that moment on, Bezalel has a job — a job that God had prepared him to do all his life, which was not to work for Pharaoh building lavish monuments to a man or false gods, but to build God's dwelling place and furnish it.

Okay, maybe I embellished the story in the Bible a little, but not the facts. What happened to Bezalel that day is what happens in the life of every church facility manager that is called by God.

Also, in the Old Testament books of Ezra and Nehemiah, God calls Zerubbabel and Jeshua to rebuild the Temple to its former glory, then Nehemiah to rebuild the wall around Jerusalem. We don't know what these men were trained to do vocationally. All we really know is that Nehemiah was the king's wine taster, not the king's general contractor. What we do know is that God empowered these men and others to step out of their comfort zone and do great things for Him.

What you do is not a job — it is a call. It is an empowered call by the Spirit of God to do something that you alone could never do. Don't ever forget this. You may never feel qualified in earthly knowledge and skill to do what you do as a facility manager, but with the Holy Spirit upon you and empowering you, God will give you the ability to do amazing things.

Facility managers have a 24/7 job; we are always on duty. As hard as that can be, it is equally wonderful to know that God has called you to be responsible for the upkeep of His house, so it can truly be "a house of prayer" and worship, a place of encouragement and refreshing for people who need a Savior. These buildings of brick and mortar are so much more than just their materials. Our church facilities are a place where God draws us to Him and then changes our lives for His glory.

CHAPTER 2
A Safe Harbor

Why Your Church Facilities Are So Important

In many coastal ports there are jetties or natural barriers that extend past the mouth of the ship channel or harbor and extend out into the ocean, gulf, or sea. These jetties or passageways keep the water calm from wind and waves for freighters, cruise ships, and fishing and recreational boats as they come and go. These manmade and natural barriers provide safe passage, quite literally providing a safe harbor for ships and boats of almost any size.

This is the principle I want you to invest in as you maintain and steward the house of God. I have heard people all my adult life say that when they come to church there is a peace that comes over them. There is a calmness they feel while in the walls of the church that doesn't exist at home.

Now, I'm not going to delve into what people are dealing with in their lives, and I know the Holy Spirit is ultimately responsible for the peace we experience. In this sinful world, there is turmoil at every bend, but the point here is that, for many people, the church serves the same purpose that those jetties do for ships as they approach land. The walls of the church become a safe harbor for people whose lives are constantly tossed about like a ship in a storm.

Today, the places we worship are so varied. We see traditional cathedrals whose spires touch the heavens, whose stained glass windows show wonderful images of scripture, and great choir lofts hold singers proclaiming the majesty of His glory. Then we drive out into the countryside and see little white churches and think about how intimate and personal worship must be, singing the old hymns with a slightly out-of-tune piano.

Then we go to the suburbs and see converted grocery stores, warehouses, and commercial buildings that have been transformed into modern and cutting-edge places of worship that hold thousands of people lifting up God's name with praise bands and young pastors preaching the word in blue jeans and untucked shirts.

In God's Word, He gave specific instructions how to assemble the Tabernacle and how to build the Temple. He held nothing back on how these places where He would be present would be built, from how the silver and gold plating would be applied, to the specific placement and details of the decorative pomegranates on the pillars. Yet, in the New Testament, we see believers in upper rooms, and homes worshiping their Lord. Recorded church history even tells of Christians fleeing down into the catacombs in order to have corporate worship.

There is no right or wrong place to worship our Lord, nor design or shape of a worship center that invites the presence of God more, but I would dare to say as facility managers, there is one constant in our places of worship we should all be mindful of.

This one constant is to make sure the church building is in as clean, neat, and repaired state as possible by service time. A major reason I have always been so committed to excellence in the way the buildings looked on a day of

CHAPTER 2: A SAFE HARBOR

worship is the first impression that people get when they come to church.

For example, what if someone pulls in a church drive and their tire hits a huge pothole? Or while walking in they step in "water" seeping up through a cleanout? Then, to top it all off, when they walk in the front door, the handle practically comes off in their hand, and they trip on a piece of loose carpet. What will they think, or how will their emotions change?

For those of us who are church members and committed to Christ, those things may not be a big deal. But to a non-believer, or someone who is hurting and desperately looking for answers in their life and might be looking for any reason to reject Christ, those bad impressions of our property might be what the deceiver uses to distract them just enough that they don't experience the presence of God.

A safe harbor. That is what God's house should always be. A place where hurting hearts can come without distractions, so God can move mightily and do great things in their lives.

I'm sure the man-made jetties that protect harbors take years to build. The same goes for our properties. Maybe the list of projects you have is overwhelming, to the point it seems useless to do anything.

Maybe your budget is stretched as thin as it can go. There is this thing my daddy called "good ol' elbow grease." If you have dirty carpet, chipped paint, and bulbs that need to be replaced, call your church buddies and ask for help. Make a pot of coffee, buy some donuts, order a pizza, and get a few people to come to the church on a Saturday morning or on a weekday evening and deep clean, straighten up things, throw things away, make minor repairs and touch up paint, or beautify the outside of the church.

Whether you have an unlimited budget or no budget, there's always a way to "spit polish" your facility for worship service. You may have to hide things in closets to get the clutter out of the entrance, or use your own leaf blower to clear the walkway up to the front doors, or spread out the working lightbulbs in the classrooms so light appears more even. There are many tricks to making things look good. I compare it to a magician's illusion. As long as people stay in front of the illusion, they are amazed. What we do every day as facility managers is to let our people see what we want them to see, the amazing side of our property.

I want to ask you to do something. Sit down and make a list, numbering the highest priority needs in your building down to the minor repairs (paint, bulbs, carpet). Now, go one step farther and divide that list into two. The first list will be projects that require professional contractors. The other list will be those things that you, your team, or volunteers can do.

If you have, let's say, forty dollars a week for discretionary supplies, go buy a can of paint and some brushes and start touching up paint scratches this week. Next week, when you have forty more dollars, take it again and go get a scrub brush for carpet and some spot cleaner for the worst stains. Then the next week, take your forty dollars and buy some LED bulbs and start replacing the old bulbs in your buildings. I guarantee people will start to notice the changes in your building, and you won't be breaking the bank. You might even be able to start replacing some stained ceiling tiles and other items.

See, you don't have to do everything at once. Do these minor projects little by little, and you will be amazed how

CHAPTER 2: A SAFE HARBOR

quickly your to-do lists will disappear, and how much better your property will look.

We will talk about budgets later, but never let lack of funds keep you from doing a project that is anointed by God. Like the song says, "God will make a way." Those seemingly impossible projects have a way of getting done, especially if prayer is employed.

That spit-shined look takes time, but remember what God has done for you and how He has changed you. I bet you didn't always look like you do now spiritually-speaking. Like the apostle Paul wrote in Philippians 2:12, our salvation is a worked-out, cultivated thing that takes time. It will take time to get your facilities the way you like it. It may even take your entire time on staff there. Don't lose hope. God is a lot bigger than all your lists and unfinished projects.

I will never forget one morning when a lady walked past me in the hallway and barely slowed down, but as she passed by she said, "I see the things you are doing to the building. Thank you." I never expected that, but she had noticed the little things that we were doing to freshen up the place.

Just keep in mind how that new family or person with a hurting heart will see your building and feel the calming effect on the storms in their life. Then, as they begin to build relationships with the wonderful people in your church and see how God is working in their lives, the building issues will be less obvious to them, but just as important.

Before we move on to the next chapter, take a few minutes to make a list of people who can help you with the projects you already made a list of earlier. List people in your congregation who have a heart for creativity or design. Think

JAMES D. JORDAN

about those who are contractors, and also think about sister churches in your area that you might be able to network with for resources (ladders, tools, lumber, etc.)

I know it's a cliché, but Rome wasn't built in a day, and it wasn't built by one person. Assemble your list and assemble your team, and God will take care of the rest.

CHAPTER 3
Getting to Know Your Buildings: The Good, the Bad, and the Ugly

In Luke 5, there is a wonderful story of four men who bring their paralyzed friend to Jesus in the hopes to have him healed. I think we can safely assume that these men were the best of friends, almost like brothers. So when they heard that Jesus was in town teaching and that people were being healed, they jumped into action and made plans to bring their friend to where Jesus was teaching. We don't know if the paralyzed friend had been that way for years or had recently been injured, but what we do know is that these men obviously cared deeply for their friend and were committed to make sure he saw Jesus.

Yes, Jesus had come to town and began to teach and share God's Kingdom plan for all people. The crowds at these meetings were so large that, unless you got there early, you rarely even got in the building. Then word began to spread of people being healed at these meetings by Jesus. The four healthy friends had to do something, and they did. They went and picked up their paralyzed friend and brought him to the place where Jesus was teaching.

There was just one big problem: they were too late to get their friend inside the building and close to Jesus. What were they going to do? His health was probably so fragile that they couldn't bring him back every day until they got him inside. Now, I know the story doesn't say this, but it only seems practical that one or more of the friends knew how the roof was constructed, and realized they could remove enough of the thatch and roof slats to lower their friend down to where Jesus was ministering.

So, working quietly and quickly, they opened up the roof over where Jesus was standing and gently lowered their precious friend down to Jesus, where our Savior acknowledged the faith they all had shown, forgave the paralyzed man's sins, and healed him. What an amazing story from the Word of God in Mark 2:1-12 and Luke 5:17-21.

So why is this story in a book about facilities management?

Because you can't do your job without a close group of people around you to help and encourage you.

You may have a great team of people hired that make up the maintenance department, work on projects, and do inspections, and/or you may also have lay volunteers who are there to help you with events, to pray for the facility ministry, to help set up chairs and tables, and do small projects. There have been times when I was ready to give up on a project or a repair when my team said, "We can do that," and guess what? They did.

The paralyzed man needed his friends' faith and friendship, plus a few muscles, and you need your facility team, especially volunteers, to support you. You should never be on your own. You need a team of people like the four friends of the paralyzed man to help you with the facilities. Remember, they are called to serve in this ministry every bit as much as you are called to lead it.

Now, go find those men and ladies who will be your facilities team, who might even have to pick you up and carry

CHAPTER 3: GETTING TO KNOW YOUR BUILDINGS

you to see Jesus do a miracle.

This brings us to the actual "Good, Bad, and Ugly" part of what you do.

As I just said, know, love, and lean on your people as they support you, but also do your due diligence and know your buildings well so you can lead well.

Know the Good Stuff About Your Buildings, Inside and Out

Study construction drawings of your buildings if you have them. Gain a basic understanding of where all the mechanical items are in your buildings. Walk around and document where water cutoffs, electrical panels, air handlers, fire alarm panels, security systems, and any other systems are located. You don't have to be an expert in every system in your buildings, just know where the experts need to go.

Learn the Bad Stuff

Learn about areas of the buildings that may not have been built to commercial grade. A lot of older buildings may have substandard wiring, plumbing, windows, doors, and non-ADA restrooms that have been "grandfathered in" by the city. Most buildings constructed before 1978 may even have asbestos that is under layers of paint, under flooring, or on ductwork.

Document and learn as many of these things as possible so that, when you do upgrades or new construction, you can make improvements that will bring these things up to code without endangering anyone. I will mention this later, but if you have the funds available, it would be great to go ahead and have a remediation company test certain areas that you are concerned about that might contain asbestos. Read ADA requirements for buildings and know the basic do's and don'ts.

Title III of the ADA Public Accommodations Publication states that churches and nonprofit organizations are exempt from any ADA regulations. Despite this, most churches attempt to follow the spirit of the law and show love for the disabled by implementing ADA requirements for their buildings to the best of their ability.

Also, keep in mind that state and local building codes must be followed by all commercial property owners. These codes often have the same, or stricter, regulations as the ADA. Even churches with older "grandfathered-in" buildings will attempt to make these structures as handicap-accessible as possible. It's just the right thing to do.

Then, Lastly, Know the Ugly Stuff

Know the ugly stuff. Know where roof leaks are located. Know which air conditioner will go out every Mother's Day morning. Know which exterior door hangs up randomly on Wednesday night and doesn't close properly when the last choir member walks out of the building.

In one of my buildings, the builders had put a water line running horizontally in a wall at about 6' high, and when we tried hanging shelves, we drilled directly through the water line. Yes, I did that…

You can keep a little book to list these ugly things. You can also mark architectural drawings, as well as keep lists of things in an online list app.

CHAPTER 3: GETTING TO KNOW YOUR BUILDINGS

In the story I mentioned from Luke 5, one of the friends obviously knew how the roof was built and was confident they could get their friend to Jesus without causing total havoc. My story may have a little conjecture, but in reality, the truth and principle here are that you have to know how your building is constructed and all its little quirky "isms."

I can promise you this: whether your buildings are one hundred years old or brand new, you will have the good, bad, and ugly. Don't think you've got a honeymoon period with a new building. Of course, new stuff with warranties is nice, but even with new builds, you've got to learn all the good stuff, find all the bad stuff, and tackle all the ugly stuff.

If things need to be updated or replaced, don't just ignore them or stick a coffee can under it to catch water. You need to discuss these things with your church administrator or committee that oversees facilities and guide them to gradually get these things put into the budget to rectify problems, because the more you know about your buildings, the fewer surprises you'll find on the morning of the Christmas musical.

Statement Regarding HVAC, Electrical, and Plumbing Repairs

I know that many of you are very mechanically gifted, and can do a myriad of hands-on projects related to HVAC, electrical and plumbing. With that being said, most, if not all states, require ANY work done on HVAC, electrical, and plumbing systems to be performed by a licensed technician. All natural gas line maintenance must be done by the gas utility provider or a licensed plumber.

There are states that will allow owner representatives (like you) to perform very minor repairs as long as the existing system is not changed or manipulated from the original design in any way. Check with your state contractor licensing board to know which projects you can and cannot perform.

Here are some examples of minor HVAC, plumbing, and electrical projects that you as the owner rep may be able to perform if your state so allows:

- HVAC filter, belt replacement, and evaporator drain cleaning or repair.
- Sink, faucet, and P-Trap replacement.
- Toilet replacement and repair.
- Electrical switch, outlet, and basic light fixture replacement.

Here is a partial list of examples of things that you can likely do without a license:

- Carpentry, millwork, and trim work.
- Drywall install, mudwork, and texturing.
- Painting.
- Flooring and ceiling maintenance.
- Door maintenance.
- Irrigation lateral line and sprinkler head repair.
- Replacing of outlet covers, light bulbs, and light fixture lenses.
- Repair and install low voltage (DC) signal and control systems such as doorbell, access control, thermostats, and cameras.

CHAPTER 4
Setting Up Schedules:
So You Don't Lose Your Mind (Or Your Job)

If you are a student of the Bible at all, two things should jump out at you when you study God's Word: repetition and lists. When our Lord Jesus taught His disciples in the Gospels, He often repeated the command or principle He was teaching. This is one way we know something is really important. Kind of like when your teacher in school wrote something on the board after telling everyone the same thing the day before. That was a clear hint that item would probably be on the next test. Then, of course, there are all the lists in the Bible.

One thing I love about the word of God is how orderly He is. God is big on lists and using them to keep straight what He is trying to impress upon us. He doesn't do this for Himself, He does it for us. Look at a few of the lists that God has given us:

- Creation: Six days with clear objectives for each day, followed by the Sabbath to recharge your batteries (Genesis 1-2)
- The Ark: God gave Noah the exact measurements and details to build the ark (Genesis 6)
- The Ten Commandments (Exodus 20)
- Principles of the Good Shepherd (Psalm 23)
- Six, no seven things that God hates (Proverbs 6:16-19)

- The Godly Woman (Proverbs 31:10-31)
- The Genealogy of Jesus Christ (Matthew 1:1-17)
- The Beatitudes (Matthew 5)
- The Spiritual Gifts (Romans 12, 1 Corinthians 12)
- The Fruits of the Spirit (Galatians 5)

These are just a few of the lists that are given to us in God's Word. One thing I know is that if God uses lists to get our attention and teach us, then it is obvious that making lists is a good thing to do in our vocational life as well.

That's what we are going to talk about in this chapter and pretty much for the rest of the book: making a list of all the things that you do or need others to do in the facility ministry.

Although this book will not delve into its specifics, you need a facilities handbook that is easily accessible to you, staff, and volunteers, that spells out cleaning, setup, and opening/closing procedures for events in it. It also should contain various lists of inspections, scheduled maintenance, supplies, contractors contact list, emergency phone numbers, and inventory. This handbook should be printed off and in a binder that is prominently accessible in your office.

Required Inspections and Permits (Required City, State, and Federal Permits)

I don't care how high-tech or low-tech you are, write down a schedule somewhere for all the inspections that will happen for your building throughout the year. The best way, of course, is a calendar. Whether it's a cloud-based management software, your phone calendar, a day planner, or laminated calendar on the wall in your office, you need to

CHAPTER 4: SETTING UP SCHEDULES

line out all the inspections that will take place throughout the year, and even set reminders a week or two in advance so it doesn't catch you off guard when it occurs at the turn of the calendar.

Here are a few to get you started. You may have more or less of these items on your list depending on what your buildings are equipped with.

- Fire extinguisher inspections: annual.
- Vent hoods in commercial kitchens inspected: twice a year.
- Fire inspections: might be scheduled by the city or random inspections by the on-duty fire department shift down the street.
- Fire alarm inspections: annual.
- Fire suppression system (fire sprinklers) and riser room inspections: annual.
- Fire alarm permits for monitoring by city: annual renewal.
- Backflow inspections: annual inspection to test water backflow devices
- Elevator and escalator inspections: annually or whenever state or local principality dictates.

Setup Schedules For Classrooms, Meetings, Worship, Etc.

This will require good communication with your staff. There will need to be either a cloud-based software that staff will access to request rooms for use, or an understanding that there only be one person who controls the church calendar, and a policy that all scheduled functions be on the church calendar with setup directions as early as possible (for example, at least a month in advance).

The need for you as the facility manager to know the schedule and how things will be set up is a very good reason for you to attend at least part of regular church staff meetings. By being present at those meetings, ministers can explain why they need a certain setup. This will also give you the opportunity to ask questions or suggest other setup options if you see a red flag raised in their requests. It is always better to catch these issues early rather than on the day of the event!

Here are some examples of what room reservations you might receive:

- Sunday School class setup: 12 chairs in a circle with table for coffee and donuts.
- Lobby coffee area setup: couches, standing tables, spot for coffee bar to be brought in.
- Sign-up table setup with cover in lobby for special events or tables for guest organizations to use.
- Afternoon meetings that would require re-setting or flipping a Sunday School class.
- Weekday setups for women's / men's / prayer / senior adult meetings (example: Tuesday morning prayer and coffee).
- Wednesday setup for student ministry, choir and band rehearsal, recovery groups, etc.
- Church-wide meals in the gym, including kitchen needs such as paper goods, etc.
- Special events: Vacation Bible School, revivals, conferences.

CHAPTER 4: SETTING UP SCHEDULES

- Picnics: some cities require permits for serving food in public areas outdoors or park reservations if you have to go off-site.
- Weddings: worship center setup, bride and groom dressing rooms, reception area setup, custodial needs.
- Funerals: encourage staff to inform facility team ASAP of any special needs, meals, family rooms, or need to reschedule contractors around funeral times.

I will mention this again later, but if construction is taking place during the week, the facilities department (aka you) needs to communicate this to ministry staff in time to find another location for any events, or to have construction crews stop work for a while, such as during a funeral or wedding.

Some other reasons it is critical for you to know room schedules is so thermostats can be set properly for events and door access schedules can be set ahead of time.

Standardized Procedure For Cleaning and Checking Restrooms During Events

This may seem trivial, but it is very important to keep the restrooms tidy during a scheduled event. Whether it's a paid custodian or a volunteer that is onsite during an event, there needs to be a standardized way to check things in the restrooms.

First, determine when the best time to check the restroom is. Between services or during breaks is not the time to spot-check restrooms. I have found that the first 10 – 15 minutes of the message (sermon) or teaching time (if classes are going on) is the best time to inspect restrooms.

Example of a checklist of quick-check items for restroom might look like this:

- Place a door sign or floor sign to block people from coming into restroom while being checked.
- Check toilet paper, paper towels, and changing station pads/wipes.
- Make sure toilets and urinals look okay.
- Wipe water off the counter tops.
- Wipe the mirror off if needed.
- Empty trash.

Remember, this is not a deep cleaning. It's only a spot check while events are ongoing. Also, it is okay to empty trash between services in public areas, children's rooms, and worship center.

Ongoing Setup Schedules (Weekly)

The next checklist I would make is for the events that are scheduled at the same time and place every week on Sunday, Wednesday, Saturday, or any other regular event. You and your team will know these setups like the back of your hand, but remember you will take vacations and have illness or emergencies pop up.

Also, you and your team may attend a conference together and need others to do regular setups, so it's extremely important that you have these schedules for your volunteers or fill-ins to refer to instead of scrambling to put together a setup list at the last second.

CHAPTER 4: SETTING UP SCHEDULES

Example of the Facilities Pre-Worship Service Schedule

- Disarm security system if you are the first to arrive.
- Unlock exterior doors and straighten mats at entrances.
- Turn on hall lights.
- Turn on lights in check-in areas and lobby.
- Unlock doors and turn on lights only in classrooms being used (follow security guidelines).
- Check thermostats.
- Check restrooms to make sure they are cleaned and supplied properly.
- Check worship center setup (chairs aligned, aisles unobstructed).
- Ensure any sign-up tables are set up as needed.
- Blow or sweep leaves away from entrances and covered drives.
- Check that setup for any one-time event is done or ready to set up later.
- Ensure areas that are not being used are locked.
- After morning events are completed, set up for events later in the day.
- Clean restroom and children's classrooms if needed for evening events.
- Lock all exterior doors and classrooms as needed.

Included with this schedule, you may also want to list where some supplies are located and how to use them, such as:

- Loading the paper towel and toilet paper dispensers.
- How to put a plastic bag (liner) in a can the proper way.
- Where to find plungers, mop bucket, and mops.
- Where tissue boxes are stored.
- Where folding tables and chairs are kept.
- What to do if someone gets sick or spills occur.

How to Use Super Sorb

There is a way to clean up bad messes and not even touch it or bend over. It's called Super Sorb.

Simply pour the Super Sorb on the mess, wait five minutes or so, and sweep into a dustpan with a handle on it. It's the greatest thing. Once I discovered this stuff, those terrible calls to come over to the children's building because someone got sick were not nearly as stressful. They're still not fun, but at least those messes are tolerable now. It's available on Amazon, Staples.com, or just ask your custodial supply company to order some. It's worth every penny. Buy it by the case!

Example of Wednesday Schedule

- Disarm security system.
- Unlock exterior doors of buildings being used.
- Make sure restrooms are clean and paper supplies are good.
- Check thermostats.
- Unlock and turn on lights for areas being used.
- After events are completed, turn off lights, lock

CHAPTER 4: SETTING UP SCHEDULES

appropriate interior doors and all exterior doors (check all exterior doors even if they were not unlocked).

One thing that you will ALWAYS need to over-communicate to ministry staff is that, if they are the last one to leave building at night (or anytime), they need to turn off lights, check exterior doors to make sure they are secured, and turn on security system, if applicable.

Preventative Maintenance Schedules

This list will be much like the earlier inspection schedule, but these are items that you should be personally responsible to take care of, whether required by law or not:

- HVAC maintenance (quarterly, semiannually, or annually).
- Air filter change (quarterly or semiannually if not done by HVAC contractor).
- Thermal testing of all electrical panels (annually).
- Landscaping sprinkler system check (annually).
- Ice machine and water machine cleaning (annually).
- Ice machine and water machine filter changes (semiannually).
- Change air fresheners in restrooms (every two months).
- Fill floor drains with water (every 3 – 4 months, to keep sewer smell and bugs out of restrooms).
- Check defibrillator batteries (every 3 months).
- Checking of expiration date on pads for the

- defibrillator (semiannually).
- Carpet cleaning (annually or as needed).
- Gym floor buffed (every 3 – 4 months).
- Exterior window cleaning (annually).
- Cleaning of gutters (roof drains) if applicable (annually, after leaves fall).
- Pretreatment of grass for weeds and trimming of trees (January or February of each year).
- Door mechanism adjustment, lubrication on all exterior doors (annually).

Employee In / Out Processing

As mundane as this sounds, I cannot stress enough how important it is that new employees are given the proper training how to get in and out of the buildings. They need to know what the keys they are getting will open, and why they have or only have certain keys.

Don't be afraid to tell someone that the reason they are not getting a key to the mechanical closets is because they have no need to be in that area. This is for their protection as much as yours and could actually protect them from being blamed for something they didn't do. Also, impress on them that the keys and key fob they receive are for them to use and not to be lent out to anyone else. Period.

Now, if you don't mind getting woken up at 3:00 am by the security monitoring company, you can ignore this paragraph. Otherwise, it is imperative that you train every new employee how to set the alarm system and how to physically lock and unlock the exterior doors. Make sure they know the security code and how to cancel it if they put in the

CHAPTER 4: SETTING UP SCHEDULES

wrong number. They also need to have your phone number so they can call you if they have a question. Tell them that if they set off the alarm to call you. They don't need to call 911 or the police station. Then you can call the alarm company and hopefully keep the police from coming out to check the property. Some cities have a certain number of times they will respond to alarms before they begin to charge you for false alarm responses.

Also, train everyone on how to dog down (unlock) exterior doors, and then lock them again. The term "dog down" is a facility buzzword that simply means to disable the locking mechanism (crash bar or panic hardware) on the door rather than actually unlocking it with a key. A lot of ministers will open doors for meetings or rehearsals after hours when you are not there.

There are times as a facility manager that you will need to strongly encourage (or almost threaten) the church staff to remember to lock the building before they leave after an event. Nothing makes my heart sink more than to walk up to the building in the morning and find an exterior door unlocked. One saving grace is that ministers will usually remember to set the alarm even if they leave a door unlocked. At least by doing that there is one layer of security, but don't you dare tell them that. Doors left unlocked can still be blown open by wind, or people can pull on them, which will set off the alarms.

Make sure that employees or ministers also understand how important it is for them to open only the interior rooms that they are using. This is especially true for the children's area. If they unlock a room to use, it needs to be locked following the event. Everything should be left as it was found, or better. Hopefully this information will help you train your people, and you won't have to learn all this the hard way like I did.

If someone tells you they have a security system at home and also know how to unlock storefront doors, they still need to be trained. Every security system keypad has its own quirky things, and I promise you that every storefront door that I've ever seen has a different feel when either locking down the crash bar or unlocking with a key. Bottom line? Everyone needs to be trained, no exceptions.

Below is an example of what a checklist might look like for employees:

New Employee In-Processing

- Make keys (as needed).
- Make key fob (this is usually done on a cloud-based software system). Be sure to keep a supply of new key fobs or cards that only you have access to.
- Train how to use security system.
- Show how to dog down doors.
- Discuss security issues related to their specific role.

Employee Out-Processing

- Make sure you or your supervisor collects the keys and key fobs from all exiting employees.
- Get keys and fob from supervisor, store keys in key box, and disable the key fob.

Just a quick word here about the key fob system. Even

CHAPTER 4: SETTING UP SCHEDULES

though your software will have the number of the fob stored in the system, I highly recommend that you keep a hard copy list of fobs and their numbers on file. The numbers on the fobs will wear off, and sometimes it's hard to locate fob numbers in the database if you have a large staff or have given out a lot of fobs over the years.

CHAPTER 5
Contractors and Vendors

Establishing a Good Relationship With Your Contractors

Contractor. Is this the dirty word in facility management? It seems that, to a lot of facility managers, dealing with contractors is the bad part of their day, and a lot of contractors feel hated by facility managers.

When I began to pray about the direction the Lord was leading me after seeing that God was moving me away from leading worship, I began to look at facilities management. When I mentioned this to my brother-in-law, who at the time was a commercial roofer, there was a long silence. He then asked if I was sure about that, because his impression of facility managers was not good. He said he found them to be demanding, inflexible, and basically want things their way or you can hit the highway.

Now, after being an actual facility manager for most of a decade, I will agree that some facility managers do have some of these tendencies, but unfortunately it is often because they have been let down by the work that vendors and contractors do. The bottom line about contractors is that they can be your best friend or your worst enemy. What I have found is that, if you address the following areas properly and show the love of Christ to them and be their friend, they will in turn bend over backwards to provide professional and efficient services to you.

Meeting a Contractor For the First Time

You may think that meeting a contractor is simply just meeting them and asking them what it will cost to do something. First of all, contractors will almost never give you any kind of price quote verbally or in person, and you shouldn't ask for one. You can mention that you need quotes as soon as possible, but hardly anyone gives immediate onsite quotes anymore.

The reason for this is that most contractors use project calculating software to figure material and labor cost. As frustrating and patience developing as it can be to wait on a quote or bid, it's only fair to give contractors the time they need to do their job the right way, so you will have a good result in your project or repair.

Contractors don't like to waste time. They want to hear a clear objective from you, see plans, and hear details so they know what to bid on. Don't show up to a meeting with just an idea in your head and nothing else. Here are some items that you will need to have prepared for your meetings with contractors:

- A clearly stated or written out list of objectives for the contractor to bid on. This is often referred to as "the scope of work" for the contractor(s) to bid on.
- A list of things that you, "the owner," will provide that contractors do not need to bid on, such as dumpsters, moving furniture out of construction zone, demo, or cleanup which volunteers will do, etc. Also, you need to disclose any contractors or trades you will use in-house or would like them to use (electrician, flooring

company, etc.).
- A drawing of any proposed plan you have, even if it's a hand-drawn sketch.
- Names and numbers of architects and structural engineers that you may have already hired or are in contract with to design your project.
- The days of the week that contractors can work onsite. Most churches need work to only be done Monday through Friday, and if a project is not completed by the end of Friday, the contractor should anticipate this by Thursday evening and work with you to clean up or isolate the area properly for the upcoming day of worship (cover things with plastic, safely store tools, and so on).

I almost guarantee that a contractor, at some point during your career as a facility manager, will ask you at the last minute if they can come on a day of worship to finish a job. If this is something you would even remotely consider allowing (my daddy would shoot me if he were alive and knew I was thinking this), make sure it is not a problem with church leadership before you say yes.

Check with the contractor or their crew supervisor to make sure it is okay for you to provide water or food for their employees on your project. Contractors usually don't mind this at all, but they like to know about it first. If a contractor is on site for several days, I like to provide one meal for the crew during a project. You will be amazed what providing a meal or snacks will do to help the attitude and quality of craftsmanship of a crew working on your church.

Ask if the contractor is bonded (state-secured funds to

cover client losses), licensed (state or federal certification to service certain equipment such as HVAC, electrical, plumbing, etc.), and insured (liability insurance for damage or losses). Don't go through the process of establishing a relationship and getting bids from someone if they are not insured properly. This includes asking a contractor if their sub-contractors are licensed and insured as well. When you prepare the bid sheet with scope of work for projects, it would be good to list these things. You also need a copy of liability insurance and any license numbers the contractor has that may help support their proposal.

This leads me to a point I will repeat again: any project that requires HVAC, electrical, plumbing, or structural changes to building should be done by a licensed, insured tradesperson.

We will discuss contracts in more detail later, but make sure any contracts you sign include proper local and state disclosure statements that list customer rights and contractor responsibilities.

Now, a lot of contractors get a bad rap about not doing a good job or not using quality materials, or not showing up when they say they are going to show up, and not finishing when they say they will be done. The most important word to remember when dealing with contractors is the word COMMUNICATION.

By establishing a clear line of communication with your contractor, hopefully most problems with time and quality of work can be limited. Yes, simply communicate EVERYTHING to your contractor and tell them to call you if they have any questions or concerns about the project.

One other thought on communication: you, yes *you*, need

to walk through the construction area every day. This may drive your contractor crazy, but remember, it's your building and they are working for you. If you see something you don't understand or like, ask for an explanation of what they are doing. To communicate efficiently to a contractor, you have to be current on the project as well.

Another thing that needs to be discussed with any contractor before a project begins is to make sure they include how they expect payments to be processed. Sometimes this wording is included in contracts. Let them know how and when you process invoices and when checks will be available or processed.

Also, clearly state whether the church writes checks on a weekly or monthly basis for services rendered. A well-established contractor will usually invoice at the end of a project or ask you to pay half before the project begins and the balance after the final punch list is complete. Occasionally contractors will ask for draws on the project throughout the project. Make sure this arrangement is discussed and agreed upon *before* a project begins. Small contractors are more likely to operate this way.

Contractors will often go exactly by the wording on their contracts, so read contracts several times, ask questions, and ask your administrator or someone with a good legal eye to also read any and all contracts to make sure everything is properly worded for all parties involved.

One of the great blessings you will have is when a church member can provide a professional service, such as electrical, plumbing, HVAC service, and more. It is always great to have a contractor that personally cares for the property like you do. There are some things to keep in mind when using church members as contractors. Even though you may know them personally, when it comes to doing business, they should be as accountable as any other contractor or vendor you hire. Acting in love, yet without favoritism, they need to be given directives, timelines, goals, and expectations. Also, never hesitate to communicate concerns about quality of work, change orders, or invoicing. This can be tricky with the dear folks that you worship and share life with, but I assure you, the work these brothers and sisters provide will be a huge blessing to you and the church.

Another thought I want to share about your contractors and vendors is to have at least one person from that company that you are on a first-name basis with. This may be the owner, the administrative assistant that answers the phone, or a tech that you can ask for each time. You will find it invaluable to have a personal connection with someone from the companies you deal with.

Facility managers, you are not a pastor. With that being said, you may be the closest thing to a pastor that a contractor will know. You may find yourself being asked theological questions by contractors as you get to know them. Don't take lightly these opportunities to allow Christ to use you as a vessel for the gospel to be shared with a contractor.

In the second greatest commandment, Jesus tells us to love our neighbors as ourselves (Matthew 22:39). Yes, contractors fall in this commandment as well. We must always treat them as we would want to be treated. Contractors deal with all kinds of people as well. Make sure that when they pull out of your driveway after a project is finished, they can't wait until you call them back for another project.

Reading Contracts

Today seems to be the age of contracts. I know I mentioned contracts earlier, but they are so important that we need to talk about them a bit more. Contracts exist not only when you first agree to a project with a contractor, but many (if not most) service providers and venders that provide a long-term service for you will also want you to sign a contract or service agreement to formalize the business arrangement.

Years ago, a man taught me that covenants (which are made between God and man) are based on trust, and contracts (which are made between man and man) are based on distrust. Please remember that. A contract is made with the thought that one party will probably break it at some point.

So, with that being said, whether you are looking over a contract with a general contractor to build a $5,000,000.00 building or the annual contract for the service on the office coffee machine, please read it all. I recommend that you even ask your office administrator or financial administrator to look it over. When it comes to contracts, the more eyes on it, the better.

One thing that will help you is to first be aware of contractor rights and responsibilities in your state. You should be able to go to your state website and look at these requirements and responsibilities.

Here is a basic list of things to be aware of in general contracts:

1. In most states, it is not required to convey property (lien) to contractor.
2. Get all the work to be done in writing, including:

- Timeline.
- Cost.
- Description of work.
- Pay schedule.
- Punch list schedule.

3. Read the contract before signing it (liability, exemption of liability, payment policies, penalties, etc.).
4. Get a list of subcontractors and suppliers that your primary contractor uses.
5. Monitor all work done personally.
6. Monitor payments (look over invoices line by line).
7. Be aware of claims by subcontractors (in other words, make sure your primary contractor is paying their subs rather than expecting you to pay the subs directly).
8. When final payment is made, obtain a release from lien with final affidavit.
9. Obtain title insurance protection and warranty paperwork on mechanical items (steel building contractor, HVAC, water heaters, security systems, restroom fixtures, etc.).

Don't ever get cornered into signing a contract quickly. Keep in mind that you are the customer, and you can take as long as you need to make sure that your rights and the responsibilities of those doing work for you are properly worded in the contract.

Contractors will often say, "If you sign the contract today, we can start next Monday, otherwise it might be a couple of weeks before we can begin." Well, that's just too bad.

Nobody hates delaying a project start date as much as I do, but a correctly-worded contract is important enough to delay things a little. Here I go getting all spiritual, but I have seen God use paperwork delays to redirect a project that was outside of His will.

"For my thoughts are not your thoughts, neither are your ways my ways, declares the LORD." —Isaiah 55:8 (ESV)

"Show me your ways, LORD, teach me your paths. Guide me in your truth and teach me, for you are God my Savior, and my hope is in you all day long." —Psalm 25:4-5 (NIV)

CHAPTER 6
Volunteers:
Manna from Heaven!

I've already mentioned volunteers some, but I really don't think most facility managers understand how much volunteers can mean to their facility ministry. We don't flinch one iota about volunteers leading our Bible study time or singing in the choir or working at VBS every summer, but so many times the idea of volunteers serving regularly in the facilities ministry is often seen as a "lower echelon" role in the church.

Let me explain a bit more. When I meet with a prospective facility volunteer, one of the first things I tell them is, "Welcome to the invisible ministry." The facility ministry is unique in that, when our ministry is humming along and everything is clean and works and set up on time, no one notices – and that is *exactly* what we want. That's why I call it the invisible ministry. Now, when the air conditioner breaks, lights stop working, things spill, or dispensers are empty... then our ministry becomes *very* visible.

As a facility manager, it's part of your job to educate facility volunteers to get past the idea that *they* are invisible. I've had people volunteer, then, after helping at an event or two, they stop serving because they just aren't seen enough, or it embarrasses them to be seen emptying a trash can. I completely understand this. It's hard not being noticed. I also know one of the most gratifying things for me is to see people enjoying a facility, not having to push trash down in a container in order to make their paper towel fit in or having to look for a chair to sit in a classroom because there aren't any in there. Encourage and exhort your volunteers to serve others with the joy of the Lord as their focus.

The best thing, and I really do mean it, is the blessing you get from your volunteers that you would never dream of. At one church, my facility team consisted of a retired truck driver, two welders, an electrician, a furniture builder, a couple of engineers, a fire inspector, and several really young strong backs.

But you know what the greatest blessing was about all of these people? They would clean up the messiest mess without blinking an eye and do things that no one asked them to do. They all had the kind of servant heart that it didn't matter what their gift or talent was, they were there to serve the facilities ministry in whatever way was needed, and that's what they did. If there ever was an A-Team, they were it, and I praise God every day for placing them in my life.

Several times throughout the gospels it is apparent that the disciples of Christ thought He was leading a movement that would allow them to have a place of high standing in the organization, but in Mark 10 Jesus pretty well settles this question:

"For even the Son of Man came not to be served but to serve and to give His life as a ransom for many."
—Mark 10:45 (ESV)

Then, of course, the evening before His own death, Christ personally washed the feet of the disciples before leading

CHAPTER 6: VOLUNTEERS

them in the Passover feast (John 13). I'm sure for the rest of their lives this act of service and love rocked their world. I know I would never get over this happening to me.

Serving in any ministry is about serving others, but it is super evident in the facilities ministry where your service to others is often unseen. Trust me here, brothers and sisters – Christ knows your heart and how you serve, and He will bless you.

So don't ever take your volunteers for granted. When you have workdays, feed them. Take them all to lunch, either individually or as a group, at least once a year. Give them a nice little something at some point in the year or at Christmas. More than anything, never stop thanking them. Thank them in person, send emails, write cards, or just call them to say thanks. Visit them when they are in the hospital and attend the wake or funeral if they lose a loved one. Your volunteers are your best resource. Period. Treat them like they are.

Now, for a bit of volunteer nuts and bolts:

1. **Keep a current list of your volunteers and their info.**
   Here's a good format to use:
   - Name.
   - Phone number.
   - Email.
   - Home address.
   - What they do for a living (and company).
   - What primary talent or certification they have (example: welder, electrician).
   - Miscellaneous info (like if they have a trailer, lots of tools, etc.).

You may be able to put some of these notes on your database, but it's also a good idea to have this list quickly at hand.

2. **Be sure to plan properly on how many people you need for a volunteer job, event, or project.** Sometimes you only need one person to help you flip a room between services. Other times, such as for the church picnic or Halloween Trunk or Treat, you'll need all hands on deck. Make sure everyone has a responsibility as well. One thing that makes people feel that they aren't needed is when they are asked to help and then aren't given good direction. Be sure to delegate well.

3. **I would recommend that you have some kind of social network tool to communicate with the whole team.** You could use Facebook, GroupMe, Slack, or a group text setup on your phone, or even an email group list so you can communicate quickly with your team if there is a need or an event that they can all help with. This is also a great way to share prayer requests within the team.

Here's maybe the best thing I can tell you about the facility volunteer ministry: don't ever scold people for not serving. Just make the need known, and God will give you the people you need to get the job or project done.

This ministry will not draw the masses, but it will draw some incredible people who serve simply to serve, and that will be a joy for you to watch as God changes their lives and the ones they serve. Volunteers really can be that manna from heaven that God provides just enough of when you need it.

CHAPTER 7
The House of the Lord:
Do you know all the parts of your building?

As this chapter progressed, it grew very, very long. I really wanted to keep all the mechanical systems in one chapter, so I chose to divide it into subchapters. I hope this will help keep the chapter not to feel soooo long, and also help you reference items easier in the future.

    7.1 Introduction to Building Systems
    7.2 HVAC
    7.3 Electrical
    7.4 Plumbing
    7.5 Lawn Sprinklers & Property Drainage
    7.6 Roofing
    7.7 Security/Fire Alarm/Fire Suppression Systems
    7.8 Exterior Safety/Parking Lots/Landscaping
    7.9 Construction Basics

7.1 Introduction to Building Systems

In Exodus 25:8 (ESV), the Lord speaks to Moses and says, "And let them make me a sanctuary, that I may dwell in their midst." In Exodus (chapters 25 – 28) God describes precisely how to build the Tabernacle. Every piece of the Tabernacle had a purpose and was to be built to a specific plan.

Your buildings are much the same way. It often takes 2 – 3 years to design, plan, and construct a building, then once you get into the building, it takes another chunk of time to learn the building, set up inspections, and establish maintenance plans, cleaning schedules, and utility efficiency schedules.

In this chapter, we will simply skim the surface of many different systems and terms you will use each day. This may be the part of the book you only refer to as needed for reference purposes. I would not blame you a bit for skipping over this chapter and coming back to it when you need to check something.

I mentioned earlier the importance of having a good relationship with your contractors, and this chapter will help you build and hone those relationships. When you have a halfway good understanding of the basic terms and principles that a contractor specializes in, you will be able to stay in the conversation, or at least understand what they are talking about.

There is no way I will cover every term you need to know as a facility manager, especially if you pursue a nationally recognized certification, but this is a good starting point. Fortunately, we have the internet, so you can always search for a term or concept if you're in a meeting and need to get a quick understanding of something. My goal is to cover the basic everyday terms you will need to know so you can communicate with a contractor.

Now, I could list everything alphabetically, but I think it might be better to list things as you will see them when you enter the buildings. As you read, I want you to imagine

CHAPTER 7: THE HOUSE OF THE LORD

yourself walking up to the building. What things do you see? What things are you supposed to see? When you walk into the building, what equipment or systems are required within a few feet of the front entrance?

Once we get into the building, then we will begin to look at things system by system. If you're needing a good nap, this may be your chapter to snooze, but I hope it will help give you a basic understanding of what is in your building.

Building Basics

Okay, imagine you are walking up to your building. You have parked in the parking lot, so let's start there. The parking lot surface should be in good smooth condition, with no uneven surfaces or potholes. Parking lot light poles should be well painted, and lighting operational (you'll have to be there at night, of course). Parking spaces should be clearly painted. Handicap parking, walkways, fire lanes, speed bumps, and ramps should all be clearly painted.

As you approach the building, there should not be standing water or mildew on the sidewalks or curbs. Signage with directions to children's area, adult classes, and worship center need to be clearly and professionally displayed. Landscaping, flowerbeds, trees, and bushes should be neatly trimmed. All painted exterior elements need to be in good condition, and there should be no clutter around any exterior door.

Now let's start talking specifically about items on and in your building.

Sconces (pronounced *SKON-sez*):
Light fixtures that could either be of the commercial security type or decorative lights on each side of your exterior doors or located in intervals around the building.

Lighting Sconces

Porte Cochere (pronounced *PORT ko-SHARE*): Term used mostly by architects to refer to a covered driveway.

Porte Cochere Example

Runners: Also called doormats, of all different shapes and sizes. You may choose to contract with a company that provides clean runners all the time at your entrances, or you may take care of them in-house with a power washer. These can be standard, indoor, or outdoor, and some companies

CHAPTER 7: THE HOUSE OF THE LORD

will personalize your mats with your church logo.

Knox Box:
This box is for fire department use only. It's a metal box (4" x 4") that is either built into the brick or bolted to the building just 2 – 3 feet to the side of the main door of the main building.

Flush Mount Knox Box

Surface Mount Knox Box

I like to use a ziplock bag and put one of my business cards inside. On the back of the business card, I put the code for the security alarm and highlight my phone number on the front. I also place a grand master key in the bag, then place this in the Knox Box.

The fire department that shows up first will need these things to open front doors and disable the security system, unless you want a new front door, which they will gladly make for you with a hatchet.

DOORS

Next, you will open your front door. What kind of doors do you have?

Storefront: Glass doors, usually with metal framing.

Storefront Example

Solid Door: These can be wood or steel and be either **solid core** (very heavy) or **honeycomb**, which is lighter.

Solid core office door with light kit

Light Kits: Long narrow window in the door (usually 4" – 6" wide x 24" tall). These are called light kits or vision kits. The screws around the frame of these light kits should always face the interior of a building or room. Office and classroom doors will often have light kits in them, and I highly recommend them for the protection of those inside the room. This is one of the first things "Kid Safe" (child abuse) consultants will recommend.

CHAPTER 7: THE HOUSE OF THE LORD

Door Locking Hardware: This usually involves a trigger button on an exterior handle or a lever-style handle. Often you have to hold the trigger or handle down to turn the key to the desired position. Be prepared to find that almost every door will have its own quirky feel when locking or unlocking. Know these well.

Dogging Down a Door: Another much more accepted way of opening doors on a public building is to "dog down" the panic hardware on the inside of the door. This involves pushing in or pushing down the panic bar on the inside of a door and using a hex key or screwdriver to turn a slotted pin 90 degrees. Dogging the door down allows the door mechanism to stay locked, but the push bar being in the down or in position allows it to be opened. This is a great security benefit, because, if a situation arises quickly where the building needs to be locked, almost anyone could un-dog the panic hardware without a key (unless the hex key is needed), and the doors would be locked. A lot of the slotted pins can be set or released with the end of a key.

Dogging Down With Key

Dogging Down With Hex Key

To quickly review, here are the basic parts of commercial doors:

Door Strike: Usually on the frame of the door; the bolt engages with it to lock the door.

Latch Bolt: The piece that engages the strike to lock the door.

Panic Bar, Assembly, or Crash Bar: Usually a horizontal push bar on the inside of the door that opens the door easily.

KEYS

Types of Keys Often Used In Commercial Buildings

- **Passage Key:** Usually opens only one door or one set of doors.

CHAPTER 7: THE HOUSE OF THE LORD

- **Master Key:** Will open most doors, though sometimes even the master key does not have access to security-sensitive areas such as riser rooms, electrical rooms, etc.
- **Grand Master Key:** Will open everything.

Basic Manufacturers of Door Keys and Different Keyways

These are only a few, not a comprehensive list:

- Falcon/Weisner (D13)
- Schlage C (D04)
- Schlage P (D28)
- Kwikset/Hillman (D12)
- Yale 8 (D03)
- Russwin

Lock Cylinders

- **Standard Cores** have a tailpiece.
- **Interchangeable Cores** are shaped like a figure 8.
- **Mortise Cylinders** are threaded on the outside and generally provide a greater level of security.
- **Rim Cylinders** are secured with screws to a plate and have a tailpiece.

While most keys similar to your home key can be duplicated at any hardware store, there is a process called restricted keyway systems that allows you to make or have keys made by a locksmith or a trained employee that cannot be duplicated anywhere except from your personal locksmith. Schlage, for instance, has a system called the

Everest 29 that is a restricted keyway system. You can also have your locksmith stamp DND (Do Not Duplicate) on each key, but in truth, if these keys have a residential style keyway, they can be duplicated.

> **Tip:** One way to save a lot of money if you want a restricted keyway system but can't afford to change every door lock is to start by only doing the exterior doors.

Thresholds or Transitions: Usually a shiny aluminum strip at the bottom of the door mounted to the floor. It serves as a good surface for the door's weatherstrip to seal against when the door closes, and also usually covers the edge or the flooring so no one will trip on the floor edge.

The transition also serves as a way for storefront doors to lock. There is a rod in the storefront door that travels down into a hole in the transition and securely locks the door at the bottom. There is usually a rod that also locks into the top of the door frame as well. This is where the transitions can be big trouble. They can get out of adjustment very easily by all the feet that walk across them or from really heavy items such as a furniture dolly with a piano on it.

When the transition becomes bent or works out of position, often the locking rod in the door will not go into the hole on the transition. Regularly checking the transitions on exterior doors is a must. When the transition is damaged and out of adjustment with the door locking rod, this can be a common source of middle-of-the-night calls from your security monitoring company.

CHAPTER 7: THE HOUSE OF THE LORD

Items That Should be Found Inside Front Entrance of Buildings

Example of front door, equipment from left to right just inside front entrance.

- **CO (Certificate of Occupancy):** A certificate from the city, which should be framed, stating the building has been approved by the city to be used, how many people can safely occupy the building at once, and that the building can be used starting on a certain date. CO's usually are good for as long as you own the building or until a major renovation is done that changes the "footprint" of the building. This should be placed above security keypad and light switch.
- **Security Keypad:** Keypad that arms and disarms your security system. You may have keypads with different codes for each building, or link them so that, if one is off, they are all off.
- **AED (Automated External Defibrillator):** A portable

cardiac defibrillation unit that should be in a box on the wall and labeled. This unit will need to be tested on a regular basis (quarterly). Defib pads have expiration dates that need to be watched. AED units in children's areas should be equipped with both adult and child-size pads in the cabinet. The batteries in these need to be checked every 3 – 4 months. The pads need to be checked for when they expire. Buildings must have appropriately-sized pads.
- **Fire Alarm Pull Station:** There should be one of these within 5' of exterior exits, with the alarm klaxon located above it.
- **Fire Extinguisher:** These should be inspected annually and will also need to be replaced or rebuilt every 7 – 10 years.
- **Disinfectant Station**
- **Poster Frame:** This just looks nice.

The following are the types of fire extinguishers you should have on your premises:

ABC Dry Chemical Extinguisher:
Located in the hallways and electrical rooms. Pin must be installed, the gauge must be in the green, and there should be a current inspection tag attached to fire extinguisher with month and year it was inspected.

Type ABC Extinguisher

CHAPTER 7: THE HOUSE OF THE LORD

Type K Extinguisher

Class K Fire Extinguisher:
Located in kitchens; also having an ABC extinguisher in the kitchen is a good call.

Place the ABC extinguisher near the door of the kitchen and the K extinguisher near the range or deep fryer so your folks know where each extinguisher should be used. There should be no physical damage to fire extinguisher, like nicks or dents.

> **Tip:** When you have to replace old extinguishers, don't see this as a waste of money. You can use the old fire extinguishers to train your staff how to use them properly.

Kitchen Hood Fire Suppression:
Must be professionally maintained and inspected.

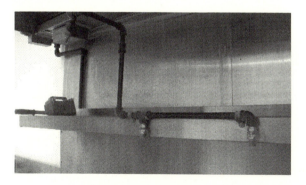

Ansel Fire Suppression Nozzles

FLOORS

Now let's talk about flooring, focusing on the styles and types.

Carpet, Vinyl, and Wood flooring

Carpet Squares: Usually 2' x 2' or 3' x 3'. These are more expensive, but easy to change if one gets damaged or permanently stained.

Long Weave or Broadloom: Carpet that comes in 12' rolls.

Cove Base: The 4" – 6" wide vinyl baseboard that is used in most commercial buildings. You can buy it in 4' lengths or 100' rolls. There is a special adhesive that allows it to be removed relatively easily and reused when doing remodeling or changing flooring.

Laminate Flooring: A vinyl-based flooring that can be laid with adhesive or clicked together on a floating moisture barrier. It can come in squares or long plank style.

> **Note:** Vinyl transition strips are often used when flooring changes (or transitions) from one surface like carpet to another surface, like vinyl.

Manufactured Wood: A very durable and more water-resistant material than hardwood flooring. It has a base layer of plywood, then a thin layer of hardwood on top.

Hardwood Flooring: The only place I would ever consider

using it in a church would be a small parlor, a conference room, or a pastor's study. I personally would never use hardwood in a church. There are so many manufactured wood and laminate styles now that look so awesome that using strictly hardwood seems like a waste of money to me.

> **Note:** In an older building with wood floors, the wide 4" boards are usually pine. Narrow 2" – 3" boards are usually oak.

Tile

Ceramic Tile Floors: Ceramic tile typically found in restrooms and entryways.

VCT (Vinyl Composition Tile): Very durable 12" x 12" hard vinyl tile that is popular in commercial kitchens, closets, and some restrooms.

Vinyl Sheet Flooring: Excellent in shower areas, custodian and storage closets, and small kitchens. More susceptible to tearing or damage from drops.

Gymnasium Floors: 5 Styles

Parquet: 6" wood squares made of four narrow strips. They are usually laid in a staggered pattern. I don't usually recommend this since moisture is not its friend.

Oak Plank: Very expensive to install and maintain. Must be refinished regularly in high-traffic areas.

Poured Urethane Synthetic Rubber: This type of flooring takes several weeks to cure. Stripes are actually painted with the same material into floor one to two days after floor is poured so that the stripes will never fade. A negative is that furniture placed on this floor must have rubber feet, and nothing heavy or with sharp corners can be dragged on the floor, as it scuffs easily. Very low maintenance, but the initial cost is high. Also, the flat or satin finish in these floors stays looking amazing over a long time. A cleaning machine is a must for these floors.

Stained Concrete: A popular and cost-saving option to floor coverings is to stain and seal the concrete floors. The basic cost can be between $2 – $4 per square foot. It will, of course, go up as you add complexity to the design. Keep in mind, this isn't the best choice for areas with small children, nor are gymnasiums the safest place for stained concrete floors. Also, acoustic consideration must to be given to areas such as worship centers.

Vinyl and Rubber Floor With Welded Seams: This flooring is for gyms or any multi-purpose facility. The flooring comes in rolls that are usually five or so feet wide and rolled out, then welded (heat used to bond edges) together. An epoxy-based line paint is used that bonds to the rubber. The picture on the next page is one of these floors that was installed in 1979. Maintenance for these floors is very simple. A light wax and buffing will easily last for 4 – 6 months. This is a very good floor in gyms. Shoe marks show up easily and floor needs to be buffed regularly to maintain a good appearance.

CHAPTER 7: THE HOUSE OF THE LORD

Rubber Floor With Welded Seams

MECHANICALS

7.2 HVAC: Heating Ventilation Air Conditioning

Your people will drive you crazy because they will disagree on everything. When designing new buildings or remodeling, you will find as many opinions on wall colors, flooring colors, parking lot layout, bathroom design, you name it, as people in the room.

Then there is your heating and air conditioning. HVAC systems are the most complicated mechanical item on your church property. That's why I wouldn't be surprised at all if your HVAC PM's and repairs are easily 10 – 15% of your facilities budget.

100% of your folks want it to work all the time. Oh, they may be too hot or too cold, but they want the HVAC system to be running. When it's not, they will be like the Israelites who complained to Moses, and you will be praying for the ground to swallow them up. Well, in love, anyway.

Once again, as you read the following, remember that I'm not trying to make you an expert. I'm simply giving you the fundamentals of the mechanical systems in your church.

HVAC TERMS

Condenser: This is the outside unit that primarily contains the compressor and the condenser coils for the system. This unit must be outside in order to remove massive amounts of heat from the condenser coils.

Coils (condenser and evaporator): The condenser coils are located on the outside unit, and their purpose is to remove heat from the system so the high pressure doesn't get too excessive. The evaporator coils on a split unit are in the air handler on the inside of the building. They are part of the low-pressure side of the system that the fans blow across to provide cool supply air to the rooms.

Air Handler: The unit inside the building that filters, cools, or heats air, then circulates it throughout the building or area. It contains an evaporator and heating coils or burners.

Expansion Valve: Controls the direction the Freon flows, separates the high-pressure side from the low-pressure side in the system

Dryer: Acts as a type of filter to keep moisture and small metal shavings from floating around in the system

CHAPTER 7: THE HOUSE OF THE LORD

Thermostat: Turns unit on and off and controls desired temperature. Many churches are installing WiFi thermostats that can be remotely accessed on a computer or via a mobile app. Some thermostat systems are pneumatically-controlled, but these are very rare in most newer systems.

3-Phase Electrical: Three equal legs of electricity. Most large roof top units (RTUs, pg. 69) use 3-phase electricity to drive the direct drive motors and compressors. This actually helps them to run more efficiently.

Condenser Fan: Blows across condenser coils to remove high temp from the high-pressure gas. When a unit is working properly, the condenser fan air exiting the condenser unit will feel warm.

Evaporator Fan: Blows through the cold evaporator or heating element and disperses air to rooms through ducting.

Register: The grille that you see in the ceiling that disperses cool or warm air within a room.

Return Air Ducts or Passages: Ducts or openings between walls which return room air to the air handler or RTU for reheating or cooling.

Relays, Circuit Boards, and Contactors: Usually located in the condenser unit, they are very sensitive to dirt, moisture, and bugs. This is one of the first things you should ask an HVAC specialist to check when a unit stops cooling, especially if the inside unit is working and the outside unit is doing nothing, or humming with nothing else going on. Circuit boards are usually in a sealed compartment on RTUs or located inside the air handler.

AC Line Sets: These are the lines that carry coolant from the condenser unit to the air handler inside the building, then return coolant to the compressor. The small copper lines are the high-pressure lines that carry Freon from the condenser to the expansion valve. These lines do not require any insulation. The larger copper lines are the low-pressure lines that return cooled coolant to the compressor. These lines must have insulation around them as they will sweat. The high-pressure (small lines) will feel hot, and the low-pressure (larger lines) will feel cool to the touch if the system is operating properly.

Drain Pan: Located under the evaporator and built into the unit and usually drains water outside or into a vent stack. Some units also have an extra drain pan suspended under the unit, because internal drain pans tend to rust out or become clogged with silt over time and then leak. The emergency drain pan is to be used only until a service tech can repair the unit's permanent drain pan.

Heat Pumps: A type of system that allows a condenser unit to reverse the flow of Freon so the hot Freon is pumped through the evaporator unit during the winter for heating rather than cooling. Heat pumps are used mostly for residential applications in moderate weather zones.

Curb: Raised platform where RTU's or condenser units are placed on roofs.

Evaporator Drains: Carry water from the evaporator drain pan outside or to a plumbing vent. It is best to vent these drain lines near the unit so the water flow will be faster. The drain lines should be wrapped with foam insulation for 10' –

CHAPTER 7: THE HOUSE OF THE LORD

12' from the unit. This will keep lines from sweating onto the ceiling. It would be a great idea to pour bleach into the evaporator drain lines of your units once or twice a year to keep them clear of silt.

Preventative Maintenance (PM): Routinely scheduled inspections occurring usually two (semi-annual) to four (quarterly) times a year on your HVAC units. Technicians will check coolant pressures, clean condenser coils and evaporator coils, adjust belts, lubricate items that require such, run electronic diagnostics, and change filters if you want them to do that. They will also make repairs as needed.

RTU: Roof Top Unit

This is a self-contained unit that is often referred to as a package unit. It only needs to be ducted to the area of the building it is heating or cooling. These units almost always need professional maintenance, even to change the air filters.

RTU (Roof Top Unit)

RTU's are perfect for setting on top of or next to a worship center or a gym. Everything can be done to the unit at one place. The only downside is that the ducting, thermostat wiring, and smoke sensors will often have to go long distances from the unit to where it is needed to cool or heat inside the building.

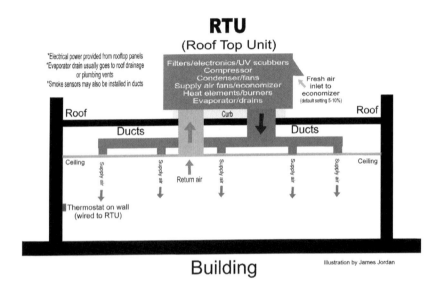

Split Unit: Two-piece unit that has an outside condenser unit and an inside evaporator air handler. These units are often a little more affordable than a package unit, and the condenser or evaporator unit do not have to be replaced at the same time. The air handler is usually close to the area it is heating or cooling and can be placed in a closet or up in the ceiling or attic area.

Filters can usually be changed by a nonprofessional. Filters can also be placed in ceiling or wall return air filter grilles for ease of maintenance.

CHAPTER 7: THE HOUSE OF THE LORD

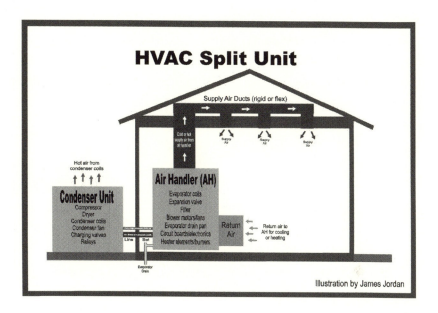

One issue I have seen with indoor air handlers in commercial buildings is that the evaporator drain lines usually have to run a long way to drain, or they build up condensation on them and drip onto the topside of ceilings. Also, if the filters are in the air handler up in a ceiling, it can be tricky standing on a ladder and changing filters.

Chiller Units

This is a system that, rather than circulating Freon or coolant to air handlers like a split system, circulates chilled or heated water or a water/glycol solution through pipes to air handlers or VAV (variable air volume) boxes. If you've ever seen the old wooden cooling towers next to or on an older building, that is a chiller system.

The cooling tower removes heat from the water that runs through the condenser side of the chiller plant. The chiller in the system is a refrigeration system which cools the water that is then pumped throughout the building to air handlers. In the winter, the water is diverted to go through a heater or boiler, then distributed through the building to the same air handlers. Chiller style HVAC systems are often used on large office buildings or large meeting venues.

The positive of a chiller system is that an air handler (VAV box) can literally be put in each room, allowing cooling or heating to be provided only to the rooms where it is needed. This is due to the fact that the water pipes usually run above the ceiling, and an air handler and thermostat can be put in each room, allowing air handlers to be daisy-chained (put in series) throughout a building wherever they are needed.

The big negative in many (older) chiller style HVAC units is that the system needs a trained technician to literally come and switch the system from cool to heat for the winter, then back to cooling in the spring. The problem, especially in southern climates, is that you may get your chiller system switched over to heating in November, then have a 90-degree day in early December, where everyone burns up. There isn't a thing you can do about this but pass out paper fans. Another negative is chiller systems are very expensive to purchase, install, and maintain.

Repairs and coolant charging during PMs will usually be invoiced separately from the PM inspection fee. When your HVAC company finishes the PM, they should present you with or email you a detailed report of all units PM'd. This is the best reason to physically place matching numbers on all your units, corresponding thermostats, and air handlers.

CHAPTER 7: THE HOUSE OF THE LORD

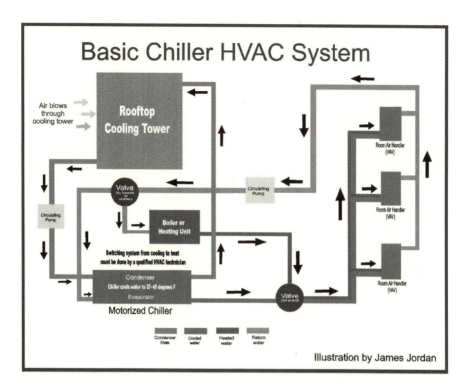

Tip: A good system I suggest is to use adhesive mailbox numbers or cut vinyl numbers for the outside units and a sharpie marker or label maker to label the inside units following this system:

- 1 on the side of the thermostat
- 1C to designate the condenser unit
- 1R for the RTU
- 1A to designate the air handler
- Then 2 would be for the next unit, and so on

The reasons I don't recommend using geographic locations to be written on units, like "east side of worship center" are (1), not everyone knows directions, and (2), it's easy to get wordy when describing a location, and (3), a good simple system is hard to beat.

These numbers should be large and located near the ID plates on the units. Be sure to ask your HVAC company to use these numbers (as well as unit serial numbers) on reports to make your job easier to identify specific issues.

Tip: Condenser units next to buildings are not to be used as a storage area.

Numbering Example

Coolant

Coolant, or Freon (which is actually a manufacturer name) as it's often called, is a stable, inert, and nonflammable gas that is used to transfer cold and hot temperature gas or liquid throughout a cooling system.

HVAC units manufactured in 2010 and later are required by the EPA to have a non-HCFC (hydrochlorofluorocarbon) type coolant **R-410A** or **Puron**. These coolants are HFC

CHAPTER 7: THE HOUSE OF THE LORD

(hydrofluorocarbon) ozone-friendly blended coolants. Units manufactured before 2010 usually had **R-22 Freon**, which is an HCFC Freon. R-22 units could be serviced with stock (new) R-22 until January of 2020. After this, they have to be charged with recycled/reclaimed R-22 (HCFC-22). After 2025, *all* reclaimed R-22 will be phased out.

If you choose to convert your older Freon over to R-410A, you will need to change out all the coolant supply lines, dryer, and evaporator coil. This is often cost-prohibitive, and I would suggest you replace the entire unit with a new system. This is especially the case since most HVAC systems have a life span of around 15 – 20 years. Anything built before 2010 will be at least twelve years old in 2021.

Air Filter Basics

There are two types of air filters: standard and HEPA. All filters use the **MERV** (Minimum Efficiency Reporting Value) rating. Standard filters use MERV ratings from 1 – 16, which tells you how effective your air filter will be at removing airborne particles.

> **Note:** A micron is 1/25,000 of an inch or 1 millionth of a meter.
>
> 0.3 microns is considered the sweet spot where air can still pass through a filter.

MERV 1-5: Basic level of filtration, usually use fiberglass and are the lowest cost.

MERV 6-8: Good for residential use, made of cloth or paper.

MERV 9-12: Mid-range filters provide relatively high quality and can filter particles as small as 1 micron (usually pleated). These are good for allergy or pet hair control.

MERV 13-16: High-efficiency standard filter and can capture particles almost as small as 0.3 micron. These filters can also include carbon-infused fiber for maximum performance.

HEPA Filters (High Efficiency Particulate Arresting) are used mostly for air purification, engine air filtration, and vacuum cleaners. HEPA filters have a MERV rating from 17-20 and are more expensive than standard filters. HEPA filters will easily capture 0.3 micron particles.

Air filters on HVAC units are usually changed semi-annually or quarterly. I have had techs tell me that a filter performs best when 30% – 70% used. This is not scientific, but it does make sense that when a filter becomes slightly used it will capture more dirt than a new filter. In other words, if your filters are clean every time you change them, you might wait a little longer between filter changes. Not too long, though. Don't let those condensers and evaporators get dirty.

> **Tip:** Metal reusable filters can also be a good investment. They can be cleaned in a commercial dishwasher or with a power washer.

CHAPTER 7: THE HOUSE OF THE LORD

7.3 Electrical Basics

The electrical system in your building is the one system that is so critical to building performance, lifespan, and safety, that I beg you to please be careful what you do without a licensed electrician overseeing your projects. I'm not saying don't do anything, but please be careful what you do when it comes to electricity.

When you make a bad mistake with plumbing, it is messy and embarrassing, but when you make a bad mistake with electricity, people die. Sure, you can learn how to change light fixtures, switches, and outlets, but every time you perform maintenance on an electrical circuit, always kill the circuit breaker you're working on before you do anything. See page 19 statement for electrical repairs you may or may not be able to perform.

Lighting and Outlet Basics

Lighting
- Light switches can be simple on/off or dimmers.
- Some switches have night lights in them when they are off, and some turn on with a motion sensor.
- Some lighting systems will have a control panel that will control several lights from one or two locations (hall, lobby, worship center, etc.).
- There are also keyed switches which are good to use in main hallways so no pranksters put everyone in the dark.
- Cloud-based WiFi lighting control is also becoming popular.

Outlets

- **15-Amp:** Has two long slots with a ground hole. Even though there is no set law for which way to install an outlet, it is a generally accepted guideline to install outlets with the ground hole down so the outlet looks like a face. The 15-amp outlet is the standard outlet for most circuits.
- **20-Amp:** Has two slots and a ground hole, but one of the slots looks like a sideways T. 20-amp outlets are best for items such as large surge protectors, computer servers, commercial coffee makers, copiers, and laminators.
- On a 15 – 20-amp outlet, the wires are usually attached with the **black wire (hot 110v)** to the copper/brass colored lug. The **white wire (common)** goes to the silver lug, and the **green ground wire** goes to the green lug on the bottom of the outlet.
- **GFCI (Ground Fault Circuit Interrupter) Outlets:** These are used in kitchens and restrooms/bathrooms near sinks. When there are multiple outlets in a "wet" area, the GFCI should be the first outlet in the series.
- **205-240 Volt Outlets and Receptacles:** These are for dryers, commercial coffee makers, commercial dishwashers, baptistry pumps, and heaters. There are several styles of outlets for 205 – 240 volt. Just be sure to follow wiring instructions when installing.

What is that big metal (green) box next to your building that has a large padlock on it? That is your electrical

CHAPTER 7: THE HOUSE OF THE LORD

provider's transformer for your building. Never mess with this box. Some electric providers put your meter on these boxes.

Electrical Transformer

You should find a box or power pole on your building where the power comes into the building. Most of the time, the electric meter will be near where the power enters the building.

You should have an electrical room in each building. Inside that room will be at least two electrical panels. One will be the main panel. This is where all the power enters the building. It will have one large breaker switch that could be several hundred amps. It may also have several smaller breakers that power your HVAC, parking lot lights, etc. It will have several 100 – 200-amp breakers for your subpanels. The subpanels simply contain all the separate circuits that go everywhere in your building to run lights, outlets, security systems, fire alarm systems, IT rooms, etc.

Panels are funny creatures. Let's say you have a 200-amp panel. Does that mean you can only pull 200 amps max in the circuits in that panel? Well, yes, but if you look at most panels, you will notice that they may have around 30 circuit breakers that add up to like 500 amps in a 200-amp panel. Why?

Well, the really simple explanation is that not all circuits are used simultaneously and therefore don't ever come close to the 200-amp total capacity.

Plus, if there are two legs of power coming into a panel, that will double the load. So, if a 200-amp panel has two 110v legs, then you can multiply 200 x 220 (110 x 2) which equals 44,000 watts. This means you can actually pull up to 44,000 watts at the same time. That's a lot, which is why panel main breakers rarely trip.

Main Electrical Panel

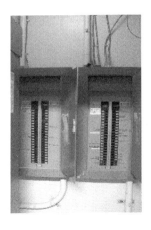

Subpanel

Most subpanels will be rated at 100 – 200 amps for regular circuits. That simply means that you can safely pull up to 200 amps of power through a 200-amp panel. The panel will have several metal conduit pipes or flex cables (solid CU MC metal clad cable) running from the panel out to the various circuits.

Your building should be grounded all the way out to the transformers (see picture on page 79).

The ground provided by the utility provider is usually adequate to handle most electrical needs with the exception of technology.

The sound system and network equipment will probably

need a dedicated circuit. This means that those items will have their own circuit that will also be separately grounded with an earth ground. Your licensed electrician will know how to install these grounds in their sleep. It basically requires them to drill a hole in the foundation, then drive a metal rod down into the ground and clamp a copper wire to that rod and the other end to the cutoff box or panel which the circuit runs to directly. This will provide what is called "clean" power to the device. This is important to remove the hum from sound systems and supply good power for servers and such.

You will find small panels at other places in your building. It is likely there is a panel in your commercial kitchen and one that operates your gym lights and goal lifts. You may also have a separate small panel for fire alarms, security systems, and fire suppression systems. There should also be a panel or, at the very least, a cutoff box near the baptistry pump and heater.

Understanding Basic Electrical Load and Formulas

The most basic electrical formulas are:

Watts divided by Volts equals Amps
(Ex: 600 Watts/120 Volts = 5 Amps)

and

Volts x Amps equals Watts
(Ex: 120 Volts x 15 Amps = 1,800 Watts)

In very simple terms:

A **Volt** is the electrical pressure of electricity (how much is going through the wire).

An **Amp** is the resistance the circuit will handle (the end user pushback by bulbs, motors, heaters, etc.).

Watts describe the speed of the current (how fast the electricity moves through the wire).
Some practical examples:

- A 110V circuit on a 15-amp breaker can handle 1650 watts. This is important because, for instance, if you have one circuit for both of your baptistry changing room outlets, then you can only have an 800 watt hair dryer in each room, or just one 1200 watt hair dryer in the ladies changing room (110 X 15 = 1650). Sorry, guys.
- If you have a portable baptistry and need to circulate the water with a pump from a 110 volt circuit on a 20 amp breaker, the circulating pump can actually pull up to around 2200 watts without tripping the circuit breaker (110 X 20 = 2200).
- For lighting: Add up the total watts of the can light bulbs installed in a children's worship area. For example: 25 bulbs X 90 watts per bulb would use 2250 watts. If you divide 2250 by 120V, you get 18.75 amps. That's a little much for a 110V 20 amp circuit, so it would be best to use two circuits for that number of bulbs. This is one more reason LED lighting is so

CHAPTER 7: THE HOUSE OF THE LORD

wonderful. 25 LEDs that have a 90 watt equivalent would only pull about 400 watts on a circuit. So, you could run all those lights and more on one 15 or 20 amp circuit.

Bathrooms and kitchen areas should have GFCI outlets. They will have a test button and a reset button on them. Really, any outlet within 6' or so of a water source should have a GFCI outlet. They are around $10 apiece, but well worth it. If you have any exterior outlets, they should also be GFCI outlets and should have a weather-proof protective cover.

Now let's discuss this little thing called LED lighting. It's time to go there. The prices of LED lighting now make it a no-brainer to make the switch to LED. Also, the technology has improved to the point that you don't have to look at that creepy blue light that the first-generation LEDs gave off.

For instance, 2' x 4' LED replacement fixtures to replace fluorescent lights are around $60 each now. Plus, with LEDs, you can put dimmers in and have whatever kind of lighting you want. Anything you have with a conventional screw-in bulb should be LED now. My wife disagrees with me. She is right on most everything else. (Love you, babe.)

The secret for me to accept and love LEDs was the temperatures you can now get. LED lighting for us facility guys runs from the blue to yellow spectrum, blue being the higher temp 5000K bulbs. These bulbs are also considered cool. Yes, cool is high and warm is low. The warm bulbs are in the 2000 – 3000K temperature range, more like a 40W bulb of old.

So, if you want to create a casual, intimate sitting area in the corner of your lobby under the stairs, you will get a couple of floor lamps and put 2500K bulbs in them. If you want to convert your covered drive-through to LED lighting, you will probably want it to have nice bright lights in the 4000 – 5000K range.

7.4 Plumbing

Plumbing for me is the "dark side" of mechanical work. Personally, I'm not a fan of plumbing. As we proceed through this section, please keep in mind that I am sharing a few terms and thoughts, but NO expertise. As I said earlier in the book, you don't need to be an expert, but you *do* need to know where the experts need to go to do their job.

To keep it simple: Call a licensed plumber to do your plumbing work! Refer to my statement on page 19 about doing any work that requires a licensed technician.

With this section, I want to give you a very basic understanding of what you will find in a plumbing system. There are three kinds of water you will deal with on your property.

1. City or utility provided treated (clean) water.
2. Sewage (black) water that goes to the city sewer system (treatment plant) or a septic system.
3. Surface drain (gray) water that runs off of buildings, property and parking lots to city provided drains, creeks, streams, etc.

CHAPTER 7: THE HOUSE OF THE LORD

I think it's important for you to be at least familiar with the order of sequence of the system components from starting point to ending point of each of these three systems:

Treated Water Supply Under Pressure (Clean Water):

(START) City or utility provided meter main cutoff valve ➡

Backflow valves ➡

Double-check valves to sprinkler system ➡

Main line to buildings ➡

Building cutoff valves ➡

(END) Inside plumbing (sink fixtures, appliances, water heaters, boilers, toilets, urinals, water fountains, etc.)

Sewage System (Black Water):

(START) Sink ➡

P-traps ➡

Toilets ➡

HVAC evaporator drains ➡

Mop sinks ➡

Floor drains ➡

Interior and exterior clean out(s) ➡

Main sewage drain to street ➡

(END) City clean out at main sewer below street

Surface Drain Water (Gray Water):

(START) Roof drains ➡

Roof runoff ➡

HVAC evaporator drains ➡

Building gutters ➡

Parking lots ➡

Property runoff ➡

Ditches ➡

Concrete or cast iron catch basins ➡

Underground drain pipes ➡

Culverts ➡

(END) City-provided drainage

CHAPTER 7: THE HOUSE OF THE LORD

Here's my very limited plumbing terms:

- **Pex:** The flexible plastic line that is now popular for running water. It comes in blue (cold) and red (hot).
- **PVC:** White pipe used for pressure and drain lines. Schedule 40 is the PVC type for supply lines. Thin-wall PVC can be used for drain lines. Make sure that if you use schedule 40 PVC for hot water lines that you purchase PVC for hot water.
- **Copper:** Copper lines are being used less and less with the advent of Pex, but if you need a good solid connection point at the wall for valves for sinks and toilets, it's still hard to beat copper connections.
- **Supply Line:** The tube or flexible line from the wall to the faucet or toilet. Older buildings had solid copper tubes with compression fittings that connected water cutoffs to a faucet. In the last thirty years, it has become much more common to use braided stainless steel or polymer supply lines.
- **Compression Fittings:** These slip over a straight pipe and tighten down, literally compressing around the pipe. They can be used without soldering.
- **Shark Bite Fittings:** These fittings are nice because they simply fit over the pipe and can be used with Pex, copper, PVC, PE-RT, and HDPE pipe. They work well if you have space issues and cannot use heat to solder a pipe. They are

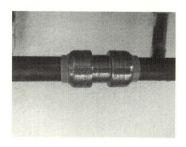

Shark Bite Connector

used to splice pipes, tee into lines, cap lines, and much more. Just be careful. They are not perfect, and I would personally hesitate to use one, then cover it up behind a wall.

- **Ball Valves:** These are inside water cutoffs that are on the wall under sinks, behind toilets, and underneath water fountains. You should be changing all of your cutoffs from the old-style knob you have to turn 10 times to a ball valve that only requires a quarter turn to turn on and off. Whenever you replace a toilet that has an old-style cutoff valve behind it, I recommend you change the valve to a ball valve.
- **Faucets:** Basic parts of a faucet are handles, stems (valve), stem seals or O-rings, stem springs, spout, and aerator. Before you replace a slow-flowing faucet, replace or clean the aerator on the end of the faucet spout. Replacing faucets is one of the easiest and best ways to freshen up the appearance of any older restrooms.
- **Toilets:** Attached to the floor toilet flange with a wax or foam/neoprene ring and bolts that lock into the floor toilet flange. Toilet fill valves and tank flapper valves are the only moving parts in a toilet. Filler valves can be controlled by a float or pressure-sensitive valve. One of the main causes of running toilets is a flush lever chain that hangs up under tank flapper valves. There are many new types of flushing mechanisms now that don't use chains or many moving parts at all. Most of these parts can be replaced easily.

CHAPTER 7: THE HOUSE OF THE LORD

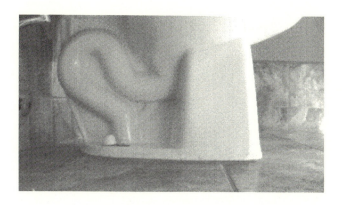

Side view of a toilet showing how the trap is built into the toilet

I would recommend hiring a plumber to change tank seals or if you have any doubts about doing plumbing yourself. Toilets over 25 – 30 years old often lose the smooth finish on the inside porcelain pipes of the toilet. When this happens, water doesn't flow properly through the toilet. This causes backups and slow flushing that will drive you crazy. There is no way to fix this except to replace the toilet.

- **Urinals:** These are wall-mounted in men's restrooms, and use a pressure-controlled diaphragm to flush. The diaphragms are not terribly hard to change but can be tricky to adjust. These should be replaced by a licensed plumber unless God gave you that magic touch required to adjust the flush pressure.
- **Water Heater:** This should be well ventilated with a vent-out if gas-heated. It should sit in an elevated drain pan. The drain pan overflow and safety valve should be piped to a nearby floor drain or a mop sink. If it's over ten years old, grab next year's budget wish list

and add a water heater to it. I'm serious.

Backflow Valve

- **Backflow Valves:** These valves basically prevent a building from doing what your 18-month-old does when they take a drink from your tea glass (aka back-washing). These are required by most cities to keep water from flowing from your building backward into city water lines and causing contamination. They usually require an annual inspection. As you can see, backflow valves aren't too pretty.
- **Vent Pipes:** These run up through the roof and tie into the sewer lines near restrooms and kitchens, preventing air locks from stopping the flow of water.
- **P-traps:** Traps are actually built into toilets and keep the smell of sewer gas from coming out of sinks, floor drains, and more. Floor drain traps need to be filled with water every few months due to evaporation. If your bathrooms have a sewery smell or you start seeing water bugs in the restrooms, that is a good sign that the floor drains are dry. All sinks should have traps under them. You can also install a floor drain trap seal that has a flapper valve that only allows drain water to go one way. These are pretty pricey but eliminate having to keep the floor drain filled with water.

CHAPTER 7: THE HOUSE OF THE LORD

- **Black Water:** The water in your sewer lines that contains waste from restrooms, kitchens, water fountains, ice machines, evaporator water from AC, etc.
- **Gray Water:** Refers to water that runs off your building roof or away from the building due to rain or sprinkler system runoff. Sometimes evaporation water from air conditioning systems can also be piped into gray water drain lines.
- **Lift Station:** Usually installed by the city in city-provided sewer system. Lift stations take sewage from a lower area and raise it up so it can keep flowing to the city sewer plant. They basically allow sewage to run uphill.

Document (Map) and Memorize the Location of the Following Plumbing Items:

Gas Meter and Regulator

- Water cutoffs and sewer cleanouts.
- Outside hydrants.
- Backflow valves.
- Water meter and gas meter.
- Riser room cutoff valves.
- Irrigation sprinkler cutoff valves and zone valves.

I would take a drawing of the property or a satellite picture off of the internet and mark all of these locations.

7.5 Lawn Sprinkler Systems and Property Drainage

Be familiar with where your double check valves (main) and manual zone valves are for sprinkler system, where the zone electric valves are located, and where your control box is located.

Sometime during April or May, get your sprinkler contractor to come out to do an annual inspection of the system. You can do this as well if money is an issue.

1. Make sure double-check valves to sprinkler zones are turned on.
2. Turn on each zone at controller and walk around and ensure there are no leaks.
3. Ensure sprinkler heads are aimed correctly.
4. Program controller as needed and set programming as required by your city.

If there are leaks or dead zones, a professional contractor may need to be hired to do repairs. Professionals have the equipment needed to find leaks and electrical problems quickly. You should be able to replace broken heads and minor leaks yourself. Electrical issues and problems with double check valves are best left to professionals.

There are several companies that sell WiFi-accessible controllers. These are great for remote access, and several brands also can be automatically controlled by weather forecasts and conditions. These controllers are usually priced from $100 – $400 based on the brand and can be installed by owner (that's you).

CHAPTER 7: THE HOUSE OF THE LORD

Exterior Property Drainage

There are three ways that water drains off of property:

Drainage Ditch

Drainage Ditches: This could be a large and wide ditch that diverts water through natural sloping around your property, or as simple as slight depressions designed into the landscaping that take water away from the buildings, playgrounds, and parking lots.

Drainage ditches in low areas where grass doesn't grow well, or where there is a chance that soil erosion could take place over time, or near culverts, are often covered with several inches up to a foot of 6" – 9" stones referred to as riprap rock.

Wide Drainage Ditch

Underground Drainage: Many properties use a wide array of underground drainage to take water away from low or high traffic areas. Channel drains are commonly used in areas near entrances, dips in sidewalks, or covered driveways. Catch basins work great in low areas in the grass. Large concrete catch basins are designed for parking lots and driveways and have cast iron grates that can take the weight of automobiles. These drains are connected to underground pipes that take the drain water to a lower area of your property, city drain lines, or to creek areas that are approved for draining by your local municipality.

Catch Basin

Outlet

French Drains:

These drainage systems are used in areas close to buildings where it would be visually inappropriate to have drain ditches or deep underground drainpipes. French drains don't drain as quickly as the other types of drains.

French Drain Outlet

They use a combination of pipes with holes in them and

CHAPTER 7: THE HOUSE OF THE LORD

gravel around the pipe to allow water to seep down into the drainpipes. French drains are usually placed just inches under the surface of the ground.

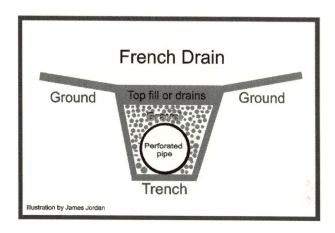

Illustration of French Drain Cross-Section

Here's a fun fact about French drains: they are not from France. A man named Henry Flagg French experimented in the 19th century with different types of drainage on his farm and came up with the idea for underground gravel and perforated pipe to drain water. That's why it's called a French drain. Not at all related to French fries or French toast (which I don't think are French either). Sorry.

Sump Pumps:
Sump pumps are used with all types of drainage systems. These pumps are usually placed at the lowest point in a drainage system to pump out any

Sump Pump

remaining water that doesn't drain off naturally. They have electric pumps in them that are float-activated. French drains are most commonly used with sump pumps, but catch basins and channel drains can also be piped to a sump pump that pumps water to lower area where water can then run off.

The picture on the previous page shows ground access (cover) to sump pump (electrical is usually close by). The sump pump pictured is actually fed by a French drain, then pumps out to street curb outlet.

Sump pumps can also be located in mechanical rooms or any area that is below grade to protect areas from flooding. If you are doing new construction and discover a spring or other water source under the new building, a sump pump system may be an option to remove water and not have to make huge changes to the building location or design.

7.6 Roofing

Since we have covered HVAC, electrical, and plumbing, let's move on to roofs. You should lock your roof access from the inside or, at the very least, keep a spring-loaded clip on the latch so no one can ever get in the building from the roof.

Regularly check the seal around the roof access hatch to make sure it is secure. Also look at the hydraulic struts that hold open the hatch to verify they are working properly on the hatch cover to ensure no one is injured by a falling hatch door. You should have warning signs posted on the inside of the roof access to alert folks about close roof edges, drop-offs, or other hazards near to the roof access.

Here's an important side note for you about roofs: the

CHAPTER 7: THE HOUSE OF THE LORD

roof is *not* a place to hang out. Get up there, do what needs to be done, and get off. I highly recommend that you be the tough guy and refuse people from going up on your roofs to look at fireworks or anything else they might get in their head to do.

Carefully climb onto the roof. First of all, do a quick visual and look around for:
- Large pools of water on the roof, HVAC drain lines that may have become disconnected from units, and roof drains that are clogged with leaves or trash.
- Electrical issues: wiring lying in water, conduit pulled loose, etc.
- Look for wind or storm damage such as TPO seams damaged, hail damage, or penetrations from debris.

Conduct a good visual inspection for obvious problems, staying clear of the edge of the roof if possible. Always watch where you step. Don't step forward or backwards without looking first.

There are several types of commercial roofs that are popular on commercial buildings:

Composite Roofs:
Shingles used on most residential roofs are referred to as composite. Shingles are rarely used in commercial roofing but will be used sometimes on HVAC curbs, near entrances, or as accent details.

Single-Ply TPO and PVC:
White or gray (usually) roofing that is rolled out and "welded" (a heat process) together. It can be shaped to fit around RTU curbs, parapet walls, scuppers, vents, etc.

TPO stands for Thermoplastic Olefin, and PVC stands for Polyvinyl Chloride. These roofing materials usually require treads for technicians to walk on so they don't puncture or slip on the TPO or PVC. Roofing membranes and adhesives need to have UV-stabilizing additives.

Built Up: This covers several types of roofing systems, but mostly refers to any type that is built up in layers from the deck. The layers usually consist of the deck, insulation, moisture barrier, tar paper or rubber membrane, tar, flashing around vent pipes, etc., then more tar and gravel or a final rubber membrane to make it waterproof.

The two most widely used are <u>Modified Bitumen</u> (see right) and <u>Tar and Gravel</u> (see next page).

Modified Bitumen Roof

CHAPTER 7: THE HOUSE OF THE LORD

Roof Coatings: High-tech polymers/epoxies that are poured or sprayed on as a top coat.

Tar and Gravel Roof

- *Chlorosulfonated Polyethylene:* Synthetic rubber is welded at seams.
- *EPDM (Ethylene propylene diene monomer):* Sheets of synthetic rubber sealed at seams with tape.
- *Cold Liquid Applications:* Polyurethane and silicone coatings applied over existing roof.
- *IB Roof Systems:* PVC-based coating.

Metal Sloped Roof Systems:
Standing-seam style of metal roofing is used on a lot of churches. This is where panels are 12" – 48" wide and link together at a seam that is about 1.5" – 3" high. This makes it very leak-resistant. There is a standing ridge about every 12".

Metal Roof With Standing Seam

Here are some basic parts of most flat roof systems:

- **Parapet Wall:** The inside of the wall that extends up from the roof 12" – 24" around the outside edge of the building. The parapet wall is where scuppers are located.
- **Cap:** Metal that covers the top of the wall.
- **Scupper:** Hole inside of building at roof level that allows excess water to run off. These are usually placed 30' or more apart around the building.
- **Flashing:** Metal that is used to waterproof transition from roof to walls or around sky lights, HVAC curbs, hatches, etc.
- **Down Spout:** Vertical chute, usually made of metal, designed to help water properly drain off the roof, usually attached to the gutters.
- **Roof Drains:** Large buildings often have roof drains that run through large pipes in the building, then down to outside or underground drain pipes. Gutters and downspouts are also used especially near areas where people enter buildings or near covered drives (porte-cochere).
- **Decking:** Metal or wood that covers the top of a building before roofing is applied.
- **Insulation:** First layer of a flat roof, usually followed by a moisture barrier. All insulation has an R rating. This R-value is a measurement of the effectiveness of thermal-insulating materials. The higher the R-value, the better a material performs as a thermal insulator. As construction codes have changed, the R rating requirement for buildings has gone up. Example:

CHAPTER 7: THE HOUSE OF THE LORD

Polyiso insulation has an R6 value for 1". R20 is the recommended minimum R-value to have on a flat roof. With this thought in mind, 4" of polyiso (4 x 6 = 24) will give you an R24 value.

Examples of Commercial Flat Roofs

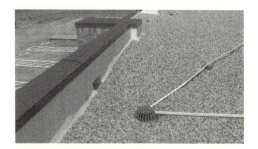

7.7 Security, Fire Alarms, and Fire Suppression Systems

Security and Safety Systems

- Security Keypad: Keypad near entrance to arm and disarm a security system.
- Door Sensors: Can be either hardwired into system or wireless.

- Motion Sensors: Also called proximity sensors; placed in hallways or other areas.

Fire Alarm Systems

Control Panel:
Where the system is turned on and off. The annual inspection tags are usually attached to the inside of the panel door. Fire inspectors will want to see these during annual fire inspections, so never remove the inspection tags. It's okay to stack them up on top of each other.

Fire Alarm Control

Fire alarm pull stations should be within 5' of exits.

Fire Alarm Pull Station   *Open Fire Alarm Control*

CHAPTER 7: THE HOUSE OF THE LORD

Fire alarm smoke detectors and sirens/strobes are located on the ceilings near entrances, at corners of halls, and in large rooms.

The monitoring for the fire alarm system will either be wired into two analog phone lines or hooked up to a wireless radio system that links to your monitoring company through an IP link transmitter and receiver.

Fire Alarm Sensor and Strobe

Riser Room: Located inside the building where water comes in directly from the city utilities (usually off a fire hydrant main line). The fire sprinkler system water comes from the large valve assembly called the riser in this room. This room should never be used as a storage area. It can have other utility equipment like electrical panels, but there should be a clear path to the sprinkler system riser.

Riser Room

Exit Signs and Emergency Lights

Exit signs should be lighted and should also have an emergency back-up battery. You will need to periodically check these by pushing a test button on the side or bottom of the exit sign.

This is something fire inspectors will check. Many exit signs also have the frog eye emergency lights (bug-looking lights on each side of exit sign) that will come on when power is lost. These should also be checked periodically.

Fire Suppression System

If you have a fire suppression system in your building, always ensure the following:
- The riser room doors must be unobstructed.
- The area around the riser must not be used for storage and there should be a clear path to the riser.
- The fire suppression system must be inspected annually. Gauges should be replaced every seven years, and sprinkler heads in walk-in refrigerators are recommended to be replaced every 7 – 10 years.
- The control panel for the fire suppression system should be in an easily accessible location near the front of your building, preferably where firefighters would enter.

Fire sprinklers are referred to as *wet* and *dry*.
- Wet means water is in all the pipes and is usually controlled by a temperature-sensitive valve in the sprinkler head.
- Dry means that the pipes in the rooms are empty and controlled by a remote valve that is opened by a sensor in the room.

A word here about your security and fire monitoring companies: I suggest that you put the monitoring phone numbers that call you in case of an alarm in your favorites list on your phone so they will come through even when you have your phone in sleep mode.

7.8 Exterior Safety, Parking Lots, and Landscaping

Outside Digging / Construction Flags

If you are planning any digging project over 12" deep, I would recommend that you have an underground utility finding company check and mark areas where you will be digging. In most states, this is a free service provided by the state.

Most states should have a direct number (such as 811 in Texas) to get an inspection, or go to usicllc.com to schedule a free inspection for underground lines or utilities at your project site.

When they come, they will mark your underground utilities with flags. This is something you need to memorize yesterday, but the APWA Uniform color codes for underground pipes and utilities are as follows:

RED: Electric
YELLOW: Gas
ORANGE: Communication
BLUE: Water, potable water
GREEN: Sewer and drain lines
WHITE: Proposed excavation site
PINK: Temporary survey markings
PURPLE: Reclaimed water, irrigation, and slurry lines

As soon as you reserve an inspection, mark your project site with white flags. Sometimes these inspection companies come out the same day even though they will tell you it takes up to two days.

Landscaping and Parking Lots

Okay, what do you need to know about landscaping? You may have twenty acres of every kind of grass and tree that can be imagined, or you may have all concrete with just a little grass on parking lot islands.

Landscaping is still important. Remember that family I spoke of at the first of the book who is looking for a safe harbor to worship? Well, your landscaping and parking lot is the first thing they see, and trust me, they see it.

CHAPTER 7: THE HOUSE OF THE LORD

Parking Lot and Playground Checklist

Here are some things to keep an eye on:

- Parking lot surface stays clean and the striping is in good condition. You will know when it needs to be re-striped based on the amount of fading or chipping.

Example of Poor Striping   *Example of Good Striping*

- Low areas are free of dirt and rocks.
- Parking lot drains well when it rains.
- Parking lot lights work (keep the timers set properly if not on a photocell) and the light poles look good (paint not chipping or faded, especially around mounting bolts).
- Fire lane paint in good condition.
- Crossing hash marks in good condition.
- Handicap parking spaces stenciled properly and the signs in front of each space in good condition and clearly visible.
- If you have corners where delivery trucks tend to run across and ruin the grass, I suggest placing large landscaping stones in those locations. For some reason, this seems to eliminate this problem immediately.
- Empty exterior trash containers regularly, and keep the

areas around your dumpsters neat.
- Keep playgrounds in excellent and safe condition. If you can't keep the playgrounds in safe functional condition, tear them down. You don't have to completely surround a playground with fencing, but the parking lot side of a playground should be fenced. During the warm months, do a wasp's nest inspection every week.
- If you have the budget to do so, I suggest hiring a parking lot cleaning service to clean parking lots at least once a year. Otherwise, you could do this with a group of people with leaf blowers on a Saturday morning. Just line them up and let them go.

Landscaping

- Mow, weed eat, and blow grass clippings weekly during the growing season. Fridays or Saturdays are great days to have landscaping done. That way things look really good in time for worship.
- Get trees trimmed during the winter months.
- Have any pretreatment for weeds done in January or February.
- Ask your landscaping company to include litter pickup as part of their scope of work and to also clear off the parking lots at the same time as when they blow off the sidewalks. This will cost a little more but will look so good.
- Trim bushes regularly during the growing season.
- If you have field areas that are not close to buildings, these can be mowed less often but should be watched

closely to ensure that they don't get out of control. You especially don't want to attract the attention of city code enforcement officers.
- Flower beds are much like playgrounds. If you can't keep them freshly planted with seasonal flowers and looking nice, get rid of them (pour concrete, lay decorative bricks, plant bushes or grass).

7.9 Construction Basics

Foundation Terms and Types

Pad: The sand or clay that is built up for the foundation of a building to set on. Most pads are laid down and compressed in layers. Core samples are sent off to a lab as layers are compacted for proper packing consistency. A geotechnical report is done before construction begins to determine how the building pad should be built up and how many piers and beams are needed under the foundation and how deep they need to go.

Pier and Beam Foundation is set up above the ground on piers and usually has a crawl space between floor framing (joist) and ground. This is used mostly for residential construction, but can be found in commercial applications. Piers are vertical supports that go several feet down into the ground. Beams are horizontal supports that run under the foundation. If a building has air vents on the outside near the ground (pictured next page), you can be pretty sure it is pier and beam.

Pier and Beam Air Vents

Slab Foundation is concrete that is poured in forms directly on the dirt pad. The slab has rebar (steel rods wired together) in the concrete to give it strength.

New Concrete Slab

Slab with Brick and Weep Holes

CHAPTER 7: THE HOUSE OF THE LORD

Building Framing

Heavy Frame Construction: Typical for large, engineered steel buildings. They can be a prefab style or a custom build that is designed by your architect. Some worship centers or gyms have large laminated wood frames that support the main structure of the building.

Heavy Frame

Light Frame Construction: More traditional or residential style of framing. This style has 2" x 4" or 2" x 6" studded walls on the exterior walls, and typically 2" x 4" interior walls. The studs are often placed 16" or 20" apart and are usually pine or light gauge steel. The wall height is based on the interior ceiling height and how much mechanical will be required to put above the ceilings or between floors. The roofs are often constructed out of wood trusses set on top of the side walls.

A historical tidbit here: Balloon framing was popular in the 1800's. This was due to large amounts of good, long lumber available. Two-story long walls would be built the height of the buildings, then floors nailed in place. Most builders moved away from balloon framing when long and straight lumber became harder to attain, and many building codes were changed to prevent balloon framing when it was determined this type of construction contributed to such disasters as the Great Chicago Fire.

Platform Construction is where each level of a structure is built separately. For example, the first floor is built, then the platform for the second floor is built and its walls set up on it. This is commonly used today.

Residential Wood Framing

Light Metal Studs on Walls with Wood Roof Trusses

CHAPTER 7: THE HOUSE OF THE LORD

Many church buildings actually use a combination of large and small frame construction where the exterior walls and roof are large steel engineered framing, then all the interior walls are small framed walls.

The above is an excellent example of hybrid-style construction where heavy frame and light steel framing is used together.

Below is a good example of a hybrid-style of construction. The middle section of the building is heavy frame construction with a custom engineered heavy steel frame.

The two wings of the building are light frame construction using traditional framing methods with wooden roof trusses set on top, then tied together with a metal roof.

If you have a steel building erected by a company that will assemble the frame and the siding, I recommend getting the steel building company to include the installation of insulation as well. All buildings should have a minimum of R20 insulation. New roofing systems require around R28 value. Insulation can be blown loosely into attic areas and rolled insulation can be used in the walls or above drop ceilings. Spray foam insulation is becoming popular but is very expensive. For flat roofs, a fiberboard-type product (ISO board) of various thicknesses is often used for insulation.

The exterior walls can be metal, wood, brick, Masonite siding, vinyl siding, stone, stucco, or just about anything else. A lot of churches use a combination of materials to save money. For example, it is very common to build a steel-sided building, then use brick to dress up the front of the building or to brick 4' all the way around to give the building a little more of a "dressed up" look.

Tilt Wall Construction

This type of construction refers mainly to concrete walls that are poured in forms on the foundation, then tilted up in place. Pouring large wall sections onsite helps to keep material transportation costs lower.

Interior Walls

A minimum of 5/8" thick drywall (required for commercial buildings) should be used on all interior walls. Water-resistant (green) wallboard should be used in restrooms.

CHAPTER 7: THE HOUSE OF THE LORD

Plywood should be used at least 8' high in gymnasiums all the way around the court. Above the drywall, I recommend using **impact-resistant sheetrock**, up to 12' – 16'. This type of sheetrock has a thin layer of plastic film in it that gives it its strength.

All interior doors should be solid core wood with steel frames. The finish on doors can be a laminate or stained/painted wood veneer. All exterior doors that are not storefront style should be metal.

Windows should be at least double pane gas-filled windows in either vinyl or metal frames. Most commercial buildings do not have windows that can be opened.

If you have a long distance between exits in a building, you may consider having one or two emergency exit windows in rooms halfway between exit doors. Your local city codes may also dictate these requirements.

Double Pane Window

Drywall Basics

Commercial buildings use 5/8" sheetrock. Most homes are built using 1/2" sheetrock. Sheetrock used in restrooms or locker rooms is usually green to designate it as water/mold resistant.

For conference rooms, pastor's offices, and choir rooms, use a soundproofing drywall and extra insulation. If soundproofing is a super-high priority for you, then specially designed acoustic walls (incorporates a "floating" wall to absorb sound) can be built to help accomplish good sound absorption. For fire walls, you can use 5/8" GoldBond or ToughRock sheetrock.

The process of finishing a sheetrock wall is called **taping and bedding**, then **texturing** occurs before you prime and paint. There are many types of texture, but the most popular in commercial buildings is knockdown and orange peel. Meanwhile, Crow's Foot style tends to be more popular in residential buildings.

Knockdown Texture

Orange Peel Texture

Crow's Foot Texture

Spanish Style Texture

Sheetrock installs sometimes leave uneven surfaces that are hard to hide by even the best mud men. On uneven sheetrock surfaces, a Spanish style wall texture works well and actually looks great when painted. This texture is also very forgiving when doing sheet-rock repair.

CHAPTER 7: THE HOUSE OF THE LORD

Reading Drawings

As a facility manager, you will need to be familiar with reading drawings. I'm just going to tell you, the best way to learn is to get a set of building drawings, or what most people call blueprints, and start looking at them and figuring out what is what.

If you have a full set of plans in front of you, there is a standardized order that plans are put together in:

- **Title Sheet and Index:** Cover page with organization (owner) name and address, architect info (name, address, seal, code ID number), and the general contractor's name and address. There will usually be an artist's rendition of the building from a perspective view of the front and the index of pages to follow.
- **Site Plan or Pilot Plan:** Shows the entire property overview of the plans, utilities, civil engineering, etc. If the project is small, this page may contain the index.

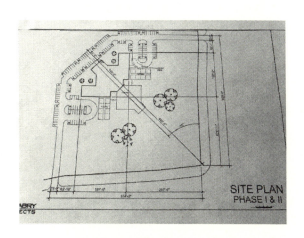

Line Drawing of Site Plan

117

Aerial Photo of Site

As you can see for yourself, the aerial (left) is almost identical to the line drawing of site plan on the previous page.

- **Landscape and Irrigation Drawings:** These plans will usually be contracted out separately by the owner (you) to a professional landscaping and irrigation company. Provide a set of site plans to a landscape and irrigation designer. Be sure you have the legal right to share your building plans with outside contractors before doing so.
- **Architectural:** Could be several pages, which would show the floor plans without measurements, floor plans with measurements, elevation (side) views of the buildings, and demolition drawings if applicable.
- **Structural:** Shows the structure of the building frame, the way the footings and piers are to be poured, how overhead load-bearing beams are designed, the way any special walls (such as acoustic) or windows are to be constructed, how cabinets and vanities are to be built with ADA specifications. This section will also have the install schedules for door, window, ceiling, and flooring finishes. It will include the roofing design and finish as well.
- **Mechanical (HVAC):** Shows the heating, ventilation, and air conditioning system design.

CHAPTER 7: THE HOUSE OF THE LORD

- **Plumbing:** Shows the plumbing system from prep stage all the way through to finish.
- **Electrical:** Shows the complete electrical plan, including lighting and outlet locations.
- **Fire Protection:** Includes the design for the fire suppression system (sprinklers) and the fire alarm monitoring.

Additional pages could be included if the architect is asked to design other systems. Most of the time these items are independently subcontracted out by the church (owner) and could include:

- Kitchen equipment
- Security system, door access system, and security camera system
- Special finishes in conference rooms, gymnasiums, children's areas, etc.
- Audio-visual equipment
- IP/server equipment, network cable pulls, WiFi design
- Playground designs
- Landscaping

One thing that you need to do ASAP is to purchase an architect's ruler. This ruler will allow you to convert the dimensions on the drawings using the scale markings (Ex: 1/8" = 1') to know and visualize the exact size of everything in a building. Architect drawings will always show the scale to use.

For the items on the building drawings, such as doors, windows, toilets, countertops, and water fountains, and mechanical items such as water heaters, air handlers, etc., you may need to download charts that will show what all of those items look like in architectural designs. You can purchase individual charts for mechanical, structural, electrical, plumbing, HVAC, finish textures, and more. These are all great resources to have.

The internet is also a good place to find many architectural symbols, but I have some examples on the next page.

One of the best pieces of advice I can give here is don't be afraid to ask an architect what a symbol means. His job is to tell you everything you need and want to know about your building. You can't be expected to know everything on the drawings — that's why we hire architects and contractors. I learned this the hard way. I didn't want to seem ignorant in front of my architect, and I should have asked more questions. Later, there were change orders that we had to do that would have been avoided if I had asked where something was or why walls and windows didn't line up. So please, ask questions and document everything.

Since many meetings with architects and general contractors (or anyone) may take place on your construction site or in a "coffee shop" setting, I suggest sending emails and texts to yourself, using a note app or keeping a small notebook as a best practice for taking notes, and keeping reminders.

CHAPTER 7: THE HOUSE OF THE LORD

ARCHITECTURAL BLUEPRINT SYMBOLS

CONCRETE WALL		STOVE	
CONCRETE BLOCK WALL		WASHER	
BRICK WALL		DRYER	
DOOR		STAIRS	
SLIDING DOOR		BATH TUB	
BIFOLD DOOR		URINAL	
DOUBLE DOOR		TOILET	
POCKET DOOR		SINGLE SINK VANITY	
DOUBLE FIXED WINDOW		SHOWER	
DOUBLE CASEMENT WINDOW		KITCHEN SINK	
FIXED CENTER CASEMENT WINDOW			

Basic Timeline For a Construction Project

Even if you have the greatest and most considerate general contractor in the world, you need to know the timeline of construction like the back of your hand. As I've said before, you must have a personal hands-on approach to any project regardless of how major or minor it is.

Step 1: Select architect, general contractor, budget, and how money will be secured (capital funding) for project.

Step 2: Determine the type of building you want to construct. The architect will guide you through this process. Building types might be a dedicated worship center, multipurpose building, office, educational, or gym/worship center. Agree to and sign general contractor and architect contracts before actual design begins. There are times an architect will do concept drawings prior to a contract being signed, but make sure you understand all legal obligations before this process begins.

Step 3: Approve design by church construction team or committee. This may be the most important step for you. Once the architect designs the building, every single inch of the plans needs to be looked at and thought over for function. Remember that anything added to the design or changed during construction will usually require a change order, which will increase the price of the project.

Think about details like:
- Water fountain locations.
- Counters and islands (millwork).

CHAPTER 7: THE HOUSE OF THE LORD

- Direction of door swings.
- TVs, directory, and direction sign locations in public areas.
- Projector and screen locations.
- WiFi router locations.
- Lighting needs.
- Kitchen design and location (exterior door with loading dock for deliveries).
- Server closet location.
- Custodial closets.
- Sight lines into restrooms, and mirror angles from the door.
- Oversize access to stage in worship center for moving large items in and out (like a piano, organ, life-size Noah's Ark for VBS, etc.).
- Convenient access to stage from green room and/or choir room.
- A green room for pastor. (Note: pastors will often say during the design phase that they don't need a green room, but it's funny that when the band has one, all of a sudden the pastors decide they need one. Just sayin'.)
- Convenient and safe access to the playground from the children's department area.
- Safe room locations for weather and security emergencies.
- Secure and controlled access to children's area and church offices.
- Types of finishes (builder grade vs. custom).
- Location of door (fob) access system.
- Access to Knox Box, security system, and fire monitor-

ing systems for first responders.
- Exterior lighting and parking lot lighting.
- Proper site drainage.

Step 4: Secure final funding. Keep in mind that your church is considered a commercial property, therefore things will be more expensive than at your personal house. Also, be aware that architects usually charge 5 – 10% design fees, and general contractors charge 8 – 20%. In nearly all cases, they charge based on the project total.

Funding for your building will probably be secured by a team of members led by the pastor of the church. They, along with a church vote, will select to raise funds before construction, implement a fundraising program, or secure funding through loans which will be paid using designated gifts, or will be built into the church budget following completion of the project.

The main thing for you to know and communicate to people is that payments to a general contractor or architect will be done throughout the construction process, so funding is a priority *before* construction begins. After all, "The wages of a hired worker shall not remain with you all night until the morning." (Leviticus 19:13, ESV)

Step 5: Give final okay on design and materials and finishes and have groundbreaking.

Step 6: Site work begins, including clearing land, building pad for buildings (ensure core testing is done properly as pad is built), clearing and excavating access roads and parking lots, and city utilities installed as much as possible.

Step 7: Building dimensions are marked off by surveyor and general contractor.

CHAPTER 7: THE HOUSE OF THE LORD

Step 8: Underground prep work for plumbing (supply and sewer), electrical, and communication is done.

Step 9: Piers, beams, and footings are poured.

Step 10: Slab forms are built and rebar is installed. Make sure the building frame support bolt studs are blocked off with framing so the contractor can come back later and pour concrete in them.

Step 11: Slab is poured.

Step 12: Frame is built, with heavy framing constructed first, then small framing.

Step 13: Roof decking and roof are installed.

Step 14: Exterior walls are dried in with plywood and insulation and wrap. Make sure your architect has used proper climate zone charts and state regulations to figure what R-values your insulation needs are.

Step 15: Exterior windows and doors are installed. If oversize items need to be brought in later, be sure to leave an opening for those items.

Step 16: Interior walls are framed up. This is a very important part of construction. This is also a great time to let your pastor bring the congregation out to the site and have them write verses on the concrete floors and the inside of the exterior walls, and pray over the buildings.

Step 17: Interior mechanical is "roughed-in" next (plumbing, electrical, air handlers, ducts, sprinkler systems, communication systems). This is the process of installing items that cannot be installed after walls and ceilings are in place.

Step 18: Drywall is installed, followed by taping and bedding, then texturing.

Step 19: Door frames are installed, then ceilings and light fixtures.

Step 20: Exterior finishes begin, such as masonry work, trim, sidewalks, parking lot striping, parking lot lights, sprinkler systems, landscaping.

Step 21: Concrete floors are stained, floor and wall tile installed, kitchen cabinets, classroom cabinets, and office cabinets installed, and painting is done.

Step 22: Finishes are done, including carpentry, plumbing, electrical, HVAC, city utilities, communication utilities, door installation, door hardware, carpet and laminate flooring installation, baseboards or cove base.

Step 23: Make sure all permits, inspections, and certificate of occupancy are completed for property.

Step 24: Complete punch list. This is a walk-through inspection you conduct with the general contractor to make sure all work is completed. GC should provide all warranties and final drawings of property.

Step 25: Final cleaning and cleanup of property are done. Furniture is assembled and set up.

Prior to the start of construction, a payment schedule with your general contractor and architect will need to be set up. The documents that you will make payments with and will need to provide to lending institutions, if necessary, are AIA (American Institute of Architecture) document **G702** and AIA

CHAPTER 7: THE HOUSE OF THE LORD

document **G703**. These documents will specifically show what work you are being charged for and the balance left on the project cost. Do not make any payments without receiving these forms. Change orders will be invoiced using the same forms, but they are usually separately invoiced.

You can find samples of both of the above forms and other applicable forms on www.aiacontracts.org, available for both educational purposes and for purchase.

CHAPTER 8
Lists, Lists, and More Lists

We've already discussed how big a deal lists are to God and how He regularly uses lists in His Word to teach us and to remind us about His ways and principles. We're going to continue with many lists that I recommend you make and keep current in your day-to-day duties. As I stated earlier, the following items really need to be in a facilities handbook that is easily accessible to staff and volunteers, especially if you are not onsite.

There are so many tools in today's world that there is just no excuse to not keep good lists of the things that will make you a successful facility manager. There are cloud-based programs, spreadsheet programs (i.e. Microsoft Excel, Macintosh Pages), and many management software programs out there. There are good to-do lists programs such as Trello. These online tools are a great way to keep up with projects, inspections, and more.

Month By Month Scheduled Inspection and Maintenance Calendar

Earlier in the book I discussed the importance of preventative maintenance and inspections, but below you will see how these could look when set up on a month-to-month calendar. Your schedule might look completely different, and that's okay.

January: Annual fire extinguisher inspection, annual roof inspection, clean gutters while taking down Christmas/Advent decorations, AED and first aid stations inspected.

February: Pretreat grass, trim trees, semiannual hood cleaning and inspection.

March: Quarterly HVAC PM, fill floor drains, replace deodorizers, power wash sidewalks.

April: Annual lawn sprinkler system maintenance and prep, AED and first aid station inspected.

May: Annual city fire inspection, semiannual water filter changes on appliances.

June: Annual city backflow inspection, quarterly HVAC PM, biannual plumbing inspections for school.

July: Annual city fire and security monitoring permit renewal, fill floor drains, replace deodorizers, playground inspection (repair and adding or tilling of wood chips), AED and first aid stations inspected.

August: Annual fire alarm and fire suppression inspection, semiannual hood cleaning and inspection.

September: Annual elevator inspection, quarterly HVAC PM, trim trees.

October: Fill floor drains, replace deodorizers, winterize exterior water hydrants and exposed pipes, AED & first aid stations inspected.

November: Annual thermal testing of electrical panels, semiannual water filter changes on appliances, purchase ice melt (or sidewalk salt) for winter.

CHAPTER 8: LISTS, LISTS, AND MORE LISTS

December: Quarterly HVAC PM, annual water heater inspection.

Contractor Contact Names, Numbers, and Emails

This may be about the most important list you keep. For starters, I would make sure that you put every contractor's contact numbers in your phone. Since it is easy to forget who does what, you might also consider putting a person's full name in the "first name" spot, and put their trade (electrician, plumber, etc.) in the "last name" spot. That way, as you are scrolling through numbers or searching for a plumber, their name will pop up when you type in "plumber."

You need a paper list as well in your desk or in a handbook somewhere in your office for others to be able to find. You can also set up a list of contractors in a cloud-based to-do list online and/or make a contractor list in your management software program.

Utility Contact Numbers and Emails

This is similar to the contractor list you already have. Be sure you can easily find the outage number to call for your utilities. Also, keep a list of city inspectors that you have met. Set up the utility app on your smartphone that allows you to report outages and monitor repairs in real-time.

Furniture Inventory

You need to keep a list of all your furniture. This could be as simple as a legal pad with each room number and the items that belong there, or it can be as involved as a cloud-based software management program to keep all your info on furniture with bar codes, warranty info, manufacturer, etc.

Tool and Equipment Inventory

This can be a simple list of hand tools, saws, yard tools, vises, drill presses, cordless tools, and the like. One important item here is to have some kind of system to remember if someone borrows tools. You might be able to just say no, but most of us soft-hearted servants who are in the facilities ministry have trouble saying no. There is nothing wrong with getting someone to sign something out in order to hold them accountable for its return, and so they know you want it back.

HVAC Inventory

This list is really important. You need to keep a list of your HVAC model numbers, serial numbers, and manufacture dates. You may also choose to record periodic maintenance inspections on this list, or note if any repairs were made or defects noticed, and if Freon (and how much) was added. This list will also be a great place to keep track of the year you plan to replace the unit. Most commercial units should start being considered for replacement around the 10 – 12 year-old period.

Exterior Mechanical Locations

The locations of water meters, water cutoffs, lawn

sprinkler systems and cutoffs, water heaters, electrical meters, electrical transformers, electrical panels, fire suppression systems, and backflow valves is very important to keep track of.

This list should also be accompanied by drawings that show locations of items, especially those that are located outside. It could also include the age of these items, which gives you a quick reference when asked by finance teams at budget time.

Contact Info and Passwords

At minimum, you need to have the following relevant contact info or access codes documented for others to access:

- Security company
- Security monitoring company
- Fire and sprinkler monitoring company
- Fire alarm maintenance company
- Door access system
- WiFi thermostats
- Camera surveillance system
- Remote lighting

This list could be kept on notes in your phone or on a piece of paper in a secure location, but the best place to keep all these passwords is in a password manager such as Lastpass.com, Manageengine.com, Get.teampassword.com, or others you may already be familiar with.

Restoration Checklist

Keep a current list of restoration companies and their contact information in case you have fire, storm, or water damage. Immediately do the following when an event takes place:

1. Turn off water/utilities to affected area.
2. Call restoration company.
3. Call insurance company.
4. Keep staff informed so that schedules can be adjusted as necessary.

> **Note:** If you have a contract with a restoration company, you will be given priority when an area-wide event takes place. Contracts do not cost anything but do bind you to using that specific restoration company.

Updated Floor Plans

This is and isn't a list exactly, but we might as well talk about this. Your floor plans are integral in your being able to accurately plan any kind of construction project, whether it's a simple door install or removal, or as complicated as a complete remodel of a building. Architects want things to be current to remove the guesswork.

No, it's not cheap to change official design documents every time you make a minor change, so come up with a

CHAPTER 8: LISTS, LISTS, AND MORE LISTS

good plan ahead of time. Any time a change is made to plans, make a copy of your official drawings and use that copy to mark changes. Be sure to mark the date and explain what was done, then place this with the official plans in the page it applies to.

After several projects have been done, or maybe every three to five years, get your architect to update the plans. This way you will be a good steward of your budget as well as keeping architectural drawings as current as possible. Keep your building drawings in an accessible, safe, and dry place.

CHAPTER 9
Project Management:
So You Really Want To Move That Wall, Huh?

Project management, I guarantee, will be the hardest thing you do, and it will also be the most satisfying thing you do. Sure, you could hire a general contractor (GC) to do all of your projects, but why? There is a good chance you have half a dozen people in your church who know how to correctly frame up a wall, install drywall, and hang a door. Then all you need to do is hire a drywall hanger/painter, an electrician to install outlets, your flooring guy to do some floor work, and voilà! Your project is done.

Okay, it's not always that easy, but there are a lot of "little" projects you and your team are able to complete. Accent walls, hanging shelving, and hanging cabinets are just a few of the projects that you and a team can do.

Now, I said that to say this: there's a ton of projects you *can't* do, but you could possibly still oversee the professionals who actually do the work.

Here's the bottom line: Do you have time to personally run a major remodel? Do you have the ability to manage such a project? Do you simply have the bandwidth in your ministry to be an in-house general contractor? It's a yes or no question. For many of us who are overseeing everything else, often the answer is "no," and that's when we hire a GC to take a project. Now, realize this as well: general contractors are not free. Their fees will usually be a 6 – 9% upcharge of the construction cost. All of a sudden, being an in-house GC looks better now, doesn't it?

If you choose to be your own GC and you have older buildings constructed before 1978, you will need to determine how much asbestos and lead you will have to deal with.

Asbestos Abatement

Before you begin any major project in a building constructed before 1978, you should have the building tested for asbestos. EPA laws enacted in 1977–78 essentially eliminated the use of asbestos in construction materials. I would recommend that, if financially possible, you have the entire building tested so you will have the complete report for any future projects.

One little nasty fact is that, even though 1978 was technically the date buildings were supposed to not have asbestos, many contractors warehoused materials that had asbestos, and these can be found randomly in buildings built as recently as 1985.

Often, if you have storm or water damage that needs to be abated professionally on an older building, the contractors may ask if you have an asbestos report for your buildings before they begin any demo.

Here are the construction materials where asbestos (or lead) commonly test positive. All but lead pipes are from materials used before 1978:

- Lead-based paint.

CHAPTER 9: PROJECT MANAGEMENT

- Lead pipes (usage by cities was stopped in the 1920's, but lead pipes in houses continued to be used, and lead in solder was used until 1986).
- Ceiling texture and ceiling tiles.
- Insulation used to wrap pipes and ducts.
- Floor tiles.
- Floor and wall adhesives (called black mastic).
- Siding used on houses.
- Roofing felt, flashing material, and shingles.
- Wallboard, drywall mud and tape, and cement board.
- Vinyl wall coverings.
- Fireproofing and acoustical texturing.
- Some tabletops used in labs or manufacturing.

To see the actual government regulatory history, go to epa.gov and type *asbestos regulations* in search window. See 40 CFR Part 61, Subpart M, Subpart L, and 16 CFR 1305 and 16 CFR 1304.

When you have documented positive tests of asbestos in your building that has never been touched or disturbed, you may choose to leave it alone. Just remember where it is located so that, when construction or remodeling ever takes place in that area, asbestos is not disturbed in any way, or abatement will have to happen first.

Abatement is not cheap. For instance, removing black mastic from a floor in a 15' x 20' commercial kitchen could easily cost $5,000 or more. Be prepared to include these costs when planning projects in areas known to contain asbestos.

There are lead and asbestos testing kits you can purchase

at local hardware stores to do your own testing. This is great for small projects or as you are pre-planning a project. Just remember, your church is considered a commercial property, so most contractors, architects, and inspectors will require professional testing reports before they proceed on most major projects on older buildings.

Several years ago, God blessed me through my church at the time with the opportunity to attain my Certified Church Facility Managers certification. As part of the certification process, I was required to write a college-level paper. I chose to write on project management and have included it here for your benefit.

Second to just simply serving people, my greatest passion in facilities management is overseeing projects. I love it. Yes, I lose my mind doing it, but it is so fulfilling to see a completed project that months ago would have been an unusable space because of its condition or layout.

Project Management

(Modified from NACFM Certification paper completed in 2016)

Knowing the Best Way To Approach a Project

Your pastor or supervisor decides to make an area larger or maybe even smaller. The children's minister decides that there are too many doors leading to a secure area of the preschool area. What do you do, and how do you do it?

First of all, keep in mind what your "normal" duties are. Some facility managers have in-house tradesmen. They have staff that can wire, lay flooring, do carpentry, and more. This

CHAPTER 9: PROJECT MANAGEMENT

is the ideal, but even if you are one of these blessed few, you need to study the project and make sure that you can do it. Or would it be more efficient and cost-effective to outsource the work?

As you begin, here's a suggested list you need to go through while making the decision whether or not to do a project in-house or hire a general contractor to oversee:

- Is the project going to require structural engineering, and will it significantly change the size or "footprint" of the building?
- Does the project require permitting from a local principality?
- Is there a maximum dollar amount your municipality will allow you to spend on a project yourself without permitting (assuming no structural changes are needed)?
- Does your municipality require contractors to be separately permitted to perform work inside the city/county limits?
- Will the project trigger regulations such as ADA that would require all buildings to be updated or changed to comply?

One suggestion at this point may be to contact a third party or general contractor that you can pay a small sum to consult with. This also might be a church member who would donate their time to consult on whether you should oversee this project yourself or hire a general contractor.

One rule of thumb I use is to make a list of everything that needs to be done to complete the project. If several trades would be required to work simultaneously, I usually get a general contractor to oversee the project. If I can divide the project into several small jobs, then I will usually hire and oversee the trade myself.

Just a quick reminder here: always be sure to check local city/county laws concerning permitting of projects before you proceed with any significant project. Also, find out at what intervals city inspectors will need to come and check the work.

Following is a list of small projects that you can usually do in-house without having to permit:

- Closing up a doorway.
- Opening up a non-load-bearing wall that does not change the integrity of the room, floor, or ceiling.
- Removing an interior window and closing up the opening.
- Painting.
- Adding lights or outlets that do not change overall circuit panel integrity.
- Installing or modifying interior windows and doors.
- Replacing carpet or flooring in limited areas (in buildings constructed prior to 1979, original flooring materials may need to be tested for asbestos prior to demo).

The Construction Project Management Success Guide, 3rd Edition[1], points out four things on page 36 that motivate

---

[1] P. Andreas. *Construction Project Management Success, The, Third Edition*. (Lexington: Self-Published, 2015) pg. 36

CHAPTER 9: PROJECT MANAGEMENT

people to self-manage a project:

1. The ability to save money on the project.
2. Self-management gives one more control over the project.
3. You get exactly what you want and you can make changes.
4. People who choose to self-manage a project gain valuable experience for future projects.

The bottom line in overseeing a project yourself quite simply is whether you have the bandwidth in time and ability to oversee the project.

Now, let us assume that you have made the decision to be the in-house project manager. What do you do next?

Project Design / Planning / Bidding

This phase of the project is the most important because this is when the flow is decided, the budget is finalized or parameters are set, and contractors are secured.

- Determine what the goals are (what you want to accomplish).
- Design and plan what you want to do (use design software such as MS Visio).
- Determine if there is a need for engineering (consult an engineer or architect).
- Determine what trades are needed and a soft budget of the project.
- Review project with your ministry staff and properties

committee or team to ensure the project is exactly what they are expecting.
- Find out if city/county permits are required.
- Put out jobs to contractors for bids (require contractors to include copies of their liability insurance, licenses, bonding, and completed W-9 forms with bid).

Construction Project Management, Third Edition[2] has a great section in chapter 7 on pages 152 – 153 describing how to put out an invitation to bid and giving bidders instructions. Invitations to bid need to include:

- The type of project.
- The size of the project.
- The location of the project.
- The date the bid is due.
- The start and completion dates of the project.
- Whether bonds or bonding is required.
- Where architectural documents can be picked up.
- Any legal requirements that need to be addressed for this project.

Specific instructions to bidders could also include the following:

- Bid due date.
- Instructions about filling out forms.
- Places to indicate fees for additional work.

---

[2] Gould, Fred. *Construction Project Management, Third Edition* (Upper Saddle River: Pearson-Prentice Hall, 2008) pg. 7

CHAPTER 9: PROJECT MANAGEMENT

- Unit prices (breakdown of pricing if needed).
- Location to deliver the bid.
- Method used in awarding contracts.
- Expected dates of award and start of project.

As an experienced facility manager, you may have contractors you have worked with for several years that you trust. I would still recommend that you get a couple of bids just to make sure your contractor covers the scope of work properly.

When finalizing terms with selected contractors, make sure you and the contractor each have a clear understanding how invoicing, billing, and payments are made. Although there is nothing wrong with setting up a payment schedule for contractors throughout the project, make sure there is a clear scope of work agreed to prior to invoicing.

If a contractor begins asking for a weekly draw after job has begun, be wary of the financial stability of their company. With this being said, there are many small businesses that routinely ask for a weekly draw and they are great at what they do. Just make sure there is good communication with your contractor in all areas of the job.

Before awarding jobs to contractors, meet with your supervisor/staff one last time to ensure the project satisfies the needs/goals they requested. When you have awarded contracts and have developed a timeline for the project, communicate this to your staff so they can plan their time accordingly. You also need to let them know that the project is getting ready to proceed and make sure there are no scheduling conflicts (conferences, VBS, etc.) that will affect the timeline of the project.

Prepping the Area

Most contractors will include cost of dumpsters, but you still need to make sure who is responsible for securing the dumpster. Another thing, as obvious as this seems, is to make sure the construction areas are ready for contractors. Move furniture, pictures, and shelves beforehand, or cover any items that will stay in the area of construction. These things seem trivial, but contractors hate nothing more than paying their people to wait for you to move things out of their way.

Tracking Progress / Checklists

The construction phase is in some ways the easiest for you, because at this point, all the specifics of the project belong to the contractors. Your job as the project manager is to make sure everything keeps moving. The best way to ensure the project proceeds smoothly and that nothing sneaks up on you is to have a way of tracking the progress of the project.

On page 265 of *Project Management for Dummies*[3], the two general types of tracking systems are discussed. First is the manual tracking system that uses day planners, physical calendars, and handwritten logs. These systems are less expensive but require space for storage of files. Also, comparing data from one document to another is time-consuming, and preparing reports is time-consuming as well.

---

[3] Portny, Stanley E. *Project Management for Dummies* (Hoboken: John Wiley & Sons, Inc. 2013) pg. 265

CHAPTER 9: PROJECT MANAGEMENT

Computer-based tracking systems, on the other hand, offer the advantage of being faster and being more efficient as far as data storage is concerned, and nice neat reports can be printed out. Also, many cloud-based programs, when updated, will sync all of your devices to assure consistent info is recorded everywhere you need. The downside of computer-based systems will always be the learning curve required to gain confidence in using these systems.

My personal preference is to "go old school" by using a white board to track the progress of all my contractors, but I am slowly being dragged into the 21st century by learning how to use some software programs to assist my projects. Spreadsheet programs like Excel and Numbers are a great tool and almost universal in use for setting up charts and tracking sheets for projects.

There are also many cloud-based apps to keep up with the status of each project and contractor. These apps also allow you to give permission to others to be able to see how the project is proceeding as well. Two of the many cloud-based "checklist" apps available are Evernote and Trello.

Even though a physical white board up on the wall in your office may seem archaic, think about this: anyone who walks by can see your progress and what is going on for the project. Not to sound egotistical, but this really impresses people, especially if you have a supervisor or pastor who wants to be in the know or has a tendency to "look over your shoulder" at what you are doing.

Setting up a project status board is always tricky, but the main thing to remember is to set it up so that it works for you. I take a blank white board and put lines on it with permanent marker. Each contractor has a row and there are common columns for every contractor.

Here is an example:

Project	Contractor	Trade	Start	Comments	Punch	Finish
Cabinets	ABC	Carpentry	11/1/20	Install complete	X	12/15/20

Change Orders

Changes in projects are another one of those processes that are not a "might happen" but are a "will happen." For example, a contractor opens a wall and finds a vent pipe that is not on the drawings. They didn't know it was there, and you didn't know it was there. Who pays for this to be moved? You do. This is a change order.

Another thing that can happen is, after the contractor begins, someone will decide another wall needs to be removed or more outlets need to be added. This is a change that very few contractors will cover in their original price.

This is why it is so important to go over the final design of the project with the staff or building team and let them okay it. Let them also know that once the project begins, you want to resist any changes and that any changes they want after project launch will cost more.

Contingency Funds

I highly recommend that you build into your project a 7 – 10% contingency fund. This will allow for unforeseen problems that arise or minor changes that need to be addressed during the project. If there are no unforeseen problems or costs that arise, these funds can be used for those change orders we previously discussed, or if nothing is added, it makes you look really good to come in under budget on the project.

Punch List

Don't let this step get "pencil whipped." Once a project is finished, you need to schedule a walk-through of the finished project with each contractor to inspect the work that has been done. Has the scope of work been completed to your satisfaction? How does it look? Is the area clean? Does the work done accomplish the desired goal? Don't let the contractor leave the job site until you are happy with their work.

Pay Bills

As far as your contractors are concerned, this is where your Christian testimony will be seen. How we pay them will be the greatest witness to them. Quite simply, be responsible all the way to the end.

Conclusion

Even when you decide to hire a general contractor to oversee your project, I would highly recommend that you closely follow the progress of the project. Ask for a copy of the timeline. Make daily contact with the general contractor. Walk through the work area at least once a day. Sit down with the general contractor on a weekly basis and let them report progress, problems, etc. Don't hesitate to ask questions.

Finally, one of the greatest opportunities to minister and love others is during projects. It's easy to be the tough guy when overseeing a project. This is actually what your contractor and their employees will be expecting. If you really care about the people working on your project and want them to see Jesus, I would impress on you to let them see Jesus through you. Take time to talk to the workers and show interest in them personally.

At some point during the project, buy lunch or provide water/snacks for the workers on the job. It's best to always inform the boss that you are doing this so they don't feel like you are going around them. Just be nice to the people who are working for you, and you will be amazed at how well the work gets done and how glorified God will be throughout this process.

In the Old Testament, Nehemiah rebuilt the wall around Jerusalem. At one point during the project, there was a real threat of attack from their enemies. Did the builders run? Did they drop everything, get mad, and attack? No, they decided to keep working and have part of the workers hold weapons to be ready to fight.

This is a great lesson for all facility managers who have to oversee major projects. The work has to be finished, even though attacks will happen. Contractors will mess up, family issues will arise. Things will come up that interfere with the job. We must stay focused on the job and at the same time watch the horizon for the enemy. This requires obedience,

CHAPTER 9: PROJECT MANAGEMENT

faithfulness, and joy in what God has called us to do. We must be obedient to do the job right and love others even when they are not lovable.

We have to be faithful to properly focus on the project, relate well to others, communicate to others, and see the project through to the end. Finally, we can be joyful in knowing that God has placed us in a wonderful position to care for facilities that will give people security and peace. Folks will know that when they and their children enter our buildings, they are entering a safe harbor where they can worship the one true God.

CHAPTER 10
Your Ministry Staff & Facilities Staff: Working With & Loving Them

One of the great joys you will have in your time as a church facility manager will be working with your ministry staff and team of associates. They will be your family away from home. Not just a church family, which they are, but also a tight group of folks you will share work and life with.

Hold on now...the first rattle out of the box about working with ministers: they are not perfect.

Are you okay?

That's right; you will find out right away that your ministry staff is human, actually more human than you would have ever dreamed. You will hear things come out of their mouths that may shock you. They will say they will do something, then they will forget to do what they said. They will sometimes just look plain lazy to you.

Guess what? They are human and sinners, with the same rebellious tendencies to God that you have. Fortunately, they are saved by the same grace of God through Jesus Christ like you. They will also be some of your best friends and helpers and confidants while you serve the Lord together.

Just realize that you are all on the same team. They may have some wild and crazy ideas that would never work in a million years, but praise God, they have you to help them figure out how to suspend a cross over the choir loft with a boat winch. No, I'm not kidding at all. That really happened.

You will love these people and do anything for them. Yes, they will drive you crazy, but you will love them like your own brothers and sisters.

One of the hardest things you will ever do as a church staff member is...absolutely nothing. What do I mean by that? Well, you will hear things that are confidential. You will sometimes be told things before even the elders or deacons know, and you will see people come in the doors of the building in tears to meet with a minister about a sensitive issue. And your response to all this? Absolutely nothing. Zip. You never saw it, you never heard it, and you don't know anything about Sister Jane coming up to the church last Thursday afternoon. This will be hard, but it's the part of ministry that no one tells you until you are facing it.

Yet it will and could be one of the wonderful things the Lord does for you. If you take this information you hear and the difficult things you see and make them part of your prayer life, giving it to the Lord and no one else, God can do things you never imagined. You might just be that instrument of prayer that could save a young student minister's career, not with your vast knowledge of teenagers, but by simply and humbly interceding in prayer.

That was heavy, wasn't it? Well, remember what I said early on: God has called you to this place at this time to serve Him and be used in ways you could never imagine.

As I also discussed earlier in the book, when we were discussing new employees and keys and all, I said your staff needs to know what limitations they have in the facilities. Well, this is a continuation of that train of thought.

CHAPTER 10: YOUR MINISTRY STAFF & FACILITIES STAFF

Your ministers, their support team, and your team only need to know what they need to know to do their job or lead their ministry. That is tough to swallow, but I promise things will go much smoother for everyone if each person on the team has access just to what they will be doing and not everything under the sun.

Sure, there will be people who think all your tools belong to them. They are your tools, and, yes, you can be a horse's rear end about letting people use them. Don't be mean, and don't always say no, but also don't let them think they have free rein in your office or storage rooms or shop. They should always ask you to borrow a tool or use the shop.

Also, ministers need to know that you have a full-time job running the facilities and that you are not their personal woodworker. If this is an issue with your staff, and you don't know how to address it, then I suggest you let your pastor or administrator gently inform them at staff meeting or in a staff email that you have several things of high priority going on (that's the truth), and they need to go to you through the operations director, administrator, or pastor if they need you for projects. This is not easy, and there can be a lot of grace given to people in this kind of stuff.

There will be staff that you are drawn to that you will never say no to, then others that, well, they will be hard to deal with, but you serve and work with them all. Depending on your environment and team, it may even be necessary to create a work order system to keep things fair, and to help you keep track of all the needs popping up around the place.

The ministry staff may not be physically working like you do, but trust me, they work, and they carry stress that is exponentially greater than your stress at times as they minister to and love people. You may go nuts trying to figure out how to open up a load-bearing wall, but that minister who's always asking you to put together furniture that a four-year-old could assemble may also be ministering and loving on people in their ministry who are about to lose their spouse and job because of an addiction.

Facility managers, close your eyes here for a paragraph. I know I have no way to enforce that, but let's just pretend, okay?

Pastors, I want to talk to you for a few sentences. Your support staff, such as the custodial crew, technicians, maintenance crew, and your facility manager, consider themselves to be a part of the staff family. Many of them have taken a job at the church, even making less money than they could elsewhere, because they feel called by God to serve at a church. Please keep this in mind, and treat them as an essential part of the staff.

This is especially important during the holiday season, for staff fellowships, picnics, or get-togethers. Please don't leave these brothers and sisters out. I would even recommend having a monthly or bi-monthly full staff meeting with all employees and ministers together. You could have coffee, donuts, a short worship time, devotional, and then a time to cover employee-relation (HR) issues if needed.

I think you will be amazed how unifying this can be for all paid employees, even part-timers and non-ministry staff, to come together as a team.

Okay FMs, you can open your eyes again. In the paragraphs above, I talked to your pastor about how important it

CHAPTER 10: YOUR MINISTRY STAFF & FACILITIES STAFF

is for all employees to feel like part of the same team. With that being said, you have to realize there are times and things that are ministry staff-sensitive, so don't get your feelings hurt or take it personally if you don't have knowledge of every decision made by leadership.

Bottom line about working with your ministry staff: love and support them, because those relationships will be the ones you will have all your life, even years after you don't serve alongside each other anymore.

Facilities Staff

Your facilities staff might be just you, you and a custodian, or an entire staff of people to assist you in maintaining the facilities. First, let's look at what the facilities or maintenance staff and line of authority might look like.

- **Pastor or Church Administrator:** This person would more than likely be the ministry staff person over all facilities.
- **Director of Facilities:** This person would be responsible for all physical locations and be the direct supervisor over all facility managers. In a smaller church, this would be done by the pastor or a designated minister.
- **Facility Manager/Maintenance Supervisor:** This person usually oversees and is responsible for the upkeep of one or more specific locations.
- **Facility or Maintenance Associate:** This is your personal assistant. This person does minor repairs (like replacing bulbs/ceiling tiles, touchup painting, minor plumbing, etc.), minor projects, furniture assembly,

multi-use area setups during week as needed, spot cleaning, etc. They may also represent the facility manager when required to do so in meetings, as well as with contractors and vendors in the absence of the FM.
- **Day Porter:** This is usually a third-party contractor-provided position that has similar responsibilities as a facility associate, but is not an employee of the church. The church bypasses normal employer responsibilities and does not provide benefits to this person, but there is usually a significant (20% – 30%) upcharge for their services.
- **Tradesperson:** This would be someone hired by the church to specifically work on HVAC, electrical, plumbing, carpentry, or other licensed trade. They would be accountable to you, the facility manager, and also assist other staff as needed and could also be given the facilities associate title.
- **Custodian:** This person cleans buildings and may do some setups as required. Custodians may also be provided by a third-party contractor or be a church employee under the facility manager's guidance.
- **Maintenance Helper:** This would be a part-time employee who is used at specific times of the year (seasonal, summer help, etc.).

For three years, Jesus Christ poured Himself into twelve people, specifically the apostles. They were not perfect, but they were called by Jesus to carry his message to a lost world after He ascended to heaven. You need to pour your life into your facility team, because they are literally an extension of

CHAPTER 10: YOUR MINISTRY STAFF & FACILITIES STAFF

you when on the job. The team needs to understand this, whether you say it verbally or not, and represent you and the church well as they serve. They should be treated by you with tender loving care.

Here are some suggestions for creating a family atmosphere and cast the vision of the facilities department and the church:

- Have weekly meetings/devotionals with the entire team. No longer than 10 – 15 minutes.
- Do lunch together sometimes (going Dutch is okay).
- Let your people see you around. Keep a pot of hot coffee in your main office, break room, or shop area.
- Monitor them, but don't hover over them. They are adults.
- Buy the department lunch at least quarterly, or take small groups to lunch on regular intervals so you can talk personally.
- Recognize their work anniversaries, birthdays, and achievements.
- Have an open-door policy. Look them in the eye when they are speaking to you.
- Pray for them.
- Go to major events in their lives (weddings, funerals, hospital stays, etc.).
- Meet and eat together with their spouses and yours a couple of times a year (Christmas, picnic, etc.).
- Have an inter-departmental communication tool (Groupme, Google+Hangouts, Tango, Voxer, WeChat, Slack) for general info like prayer requests, announcements, a good clean joke, and just overall

good communication.
- Make sure your team knows you understand how important their family is, and that if they need to attend something for family, their hours can be modified or made up later, or that vacation/personal days can be taken without any problem.
- Get their input on policy changes or work changes. Listen to their ideas, then pass along the good ones.
- Let your team see you doing the same things they do periodically (occasionally assign a maintenance project to yourself, stop and clean up a mess, jump in and help if several are needed for a group project, etc.). They don't want you around all the time, but if you are willing to do what they do, they will appreciate your leadership even more.

The people you hire (or the ones who are already on staff when you come to the job) want you to be successful, and that is why you will want them to be successful as well. If someone has been there a while, change will be hard, but if you treat them right and support them, then they will support you. Don't hesitate to make good changes. Be honest and transparent with your team, but keep in mind that your team may not need to know every detail of every issue you are dealing with.

Before we move on from this topic of personnel, I want to mention two of the hardest things you will ever do as a manager of people and as a servant leader. The first is when you have to terminate someone from your team, and the second is when you promote a team member over another.

Unfortunately, I have seen the worst of both of these. I

CHAPTER 10: YOUR MINISTRY STAFF & FACILITIES STAFF

have seen some churches that would never fire anyone, or even churches that would fire someone with no notice at all. Now, let me be clear: there is no good way to let someone go. I'm going to give you some suggestions, but there is no sure way to navigate the termination of someone without hurting feelings. Please be sensitive to your team members' personalities, as they will all react differently to the disciplinary process.

When team members are under-performing or other issues arise:

- Pray about how to approach someone who is not performing their job well.
- The only time to fire someone without some kind of notice is when there is a moral, ethical, or legal issue involved. Have good, clear documentation for this.
- Talk to an employee (never in a confrontational tone) at least twice about rectifying the work issues before terminating them. Most of the time, when someone realizes they are on the fence with their job, they will actively look for another job. At the end of each meeting, give them a hard copy of what you discussed, and both of you sign and date it. You keep a copy as well.
- Document every meeting you have with them concerning their job performance. This is a good reason to do performance reviews with all team members at least annually.
- Communicate your team member's deficiencies and reasons for termination with your supervisor or administrator first. There may be church-wide ramifications to

terminating a team member that you are unaware of.
- If the person has tenure (more than two years is my suggestion) on the team, consider some type of severance compensation. This will show grace in the midst of justice.

When deciding to promote a team member, remember the following:

- Pray about the promotion before you begin.
- Even if you are pretty sure of who will be promoted, give other team members a chance to apply for the position.
- Develop a fair and equitable way to notify, test, interview, and select promotions.
- Get other non-department employees or ministers to help you with the selection process to have an "outsiders" perspective.
- Once you have announced that team members are being considered for promotion, do not discuss the promotion privately with any of the candidates except to answer basic logistical questions. This is when you definitely need to socialize with several people rather than just a candidate alone. You must do your best to display neutrality through this process.
- When you have decided who will be promoted, first notify the one selected, and once they have accepted the job, then immediately notify the other candidates for the position. Then, as soon as possible (hopefully the next morning), announce to the entire team in person the decision that has been made. Don't send

CHAPTER 10: YOUR MINISTRY STAFF & FACILITIES STAFF

out an email.

These types of decisions are when your team seeing Christ in you is most critical. If you stay centered on Jesus in all you do, your team members will love you and understand your heart. I hope this discussion about dealing with difficult personnel decisions is helpful, because I wish I had heard things like these when I was younger. As I said earlier, your team members, like the ministry staff, will be like family to you. Respect them and love them as yourself.

I've often wondered, how in the world did Jesus decide who went with him to the Transfiguration? How hard was it for Him to pick Peter, James, and John over the rest? Also, the night before Jesus died on the cross, he treated Judas with nothing but love and respect, washing his feet along with the rest even though he knew what Judas was about to do. Only Jesus in eternity will be able to explain these things to us, but Jesus always gives us the perfect benchmark to shoot for in working with others, serving others, and leading others.

CHAPTER 11
Tools That Every Facility Manager Needs: Yes, Real Tools!

Oh boy, oh boy, oh boy! I love my tools, and I hope you will love your tools, too. You know why every person should love tools? Because our Savior was the carpenter from Nazareth. He spent his childhood sitting underneath Joseph's workbench, breathing sawdust, and I just know, as He became a man, He must have been an expert craftsman as well. After all, He did help create the heavens, didn't He?

As Jesus took His tools and made beautiful and functional furniture, we too need to take our hand and power tools and give God the glory He deserves. You may be laughing at my feelings about tools, but I'm dead serious.

I'm sure some old, salty craftsman has often said, "You are only as good as your tools." Now, let me be clear: sometimes our limited budgets won't allow us to buy the most expensive tools, but if you'll value your tools and take care of them, they will last and will do the job they were built to do.

Every facility budget is different. As I just mentioned, maybe your budget doesn't allow for a lot of expenditure on tools, but I hope you will buy a few tools to keep in your office and a few cordless power tools to do some projects.

The following is a basic list of the tools I have used and would recommend you have close at hand. I put an asterisk (*) at the end of each bullet point or item I would consider a priority:

Hand Tools

- Set of metric and SAE (standard) sockets with ratchet and extensions (I would have 1/4" and 3/8" sets). *
- Full set of screwdrivers. *
- Standard carpenter's hammer, ball peen hammer, sledgehammer, rubber mallet. *
- 2 – 3 sizes of adjustable wrenches. *
- 2 – 3 sizes of adjustable pliers such as channel lock. *
- Spanner wrench, copper pipe cutter, PVC pipe cutter.
- 2 – 3 sizes of pipe wrenches.
- Hacksaw with extra blades. *
- Sheetrock saw. *
- Utility knife (box cutter) with extra blades. *
- Levels: 10", 24", 48". *
- Carpenter's square 24" x 16", 7" speed square, Swanson tool machinist square. *
- Tape measure, metal 36" ruler, micrometer. *
- Tin snips.
- Electrical tools: linesmen pliers, wire cutter, wire strippers, needle-nose pliers. *
- Work Mate portable work bench.
- Various sizes of clamps for gluing wood, etc.

Safety Equipment*

- Work gloves, rubber gloves, latex gloves.
- Safety glasses, shop apron.
- ABC fire extinguisher to carry to work areas when needed.
- Yellow caution tape.
- Traffic cones for blocking off areas if you are working in the parking lot.

CHAPTER 11: TOOLS THAT EVERY FACILITY MANAGER NEEDS

- 12 bags (minimum) of ice melt to use on cold, icy days.

Power Tools
- Corded hand tools*: drill, 7" circular saw, router, hand grinder, Sawzall (reciprocating saw), Dremel tool, palm sander.
- Corded shop power tools: drill press, bench grinder, table saw, 10' – 12' miter (chop) saw, shop vac.
- Cordless hand tools*: drill, circular saw, Sawzall, jigsaw, leaf blower, screwdriver.
- Full set of drill bits*, set of router bids, set of paddle bits, set of hole saws from 1" – 4".

Ladders
- 4' stepladder with tool platform for each building*, 6' stepladder*, 8' stepladder*, 10' stepladder, 16' – 20' extension ladder*, multi-ladder, small scaffolding on wheels

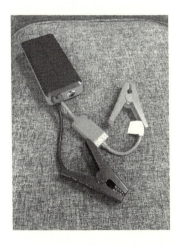

Car Booster Pack

Electronic Tools / Accessories
- Laser level, which is great for hanging posters, etc.
- Laser measuring tool.
- Volt ohmmeter.
- Dual-range current tester. *
- Stud finder. *
- Car battery booster pack (or jumper cables). *
- Circuit breaker tester.
- Plug-in outlet tester. *

- Infrared (laser) thermometer (for checking air temp at HVAC register.
- Infrared thermal imager (camera).
- Air quality meter.

Box of Miscellaneous Hardware*
- Various sizes of nails.
- Various sizes of screws.
- Various sizes of bolts and nuts.
- Electrical tape, electrical wire nuts.

If you have the space, I would recommend you keep some basic materials and tools for repairing drywall, such as:

- Drywall mesh tape.
- Medium-size tub of drywall mud.
- 4" and 6" joint knife.
- Sanding block and 80 grit sandpaper.
- Texturing brush.

Other Handy Items:
- Multipacks of sandpaper.
- Several 5-gallon buckets.
- Shop rags and bag of white (painting) rags.
- Hand cleaner.
- Mineral spirits and paint thinner (should be kept outside in a storage building or shop).
- Plastic drop cloth.
- Painter's tape, masking tape, clear package tape.
- Duct tape.
- Spool of craft wire and .032 (16 gauge) wire.

CHAPTER 11: TOOLS THAT EVERY FACILITY MANAGER NEEDS

- Disposable 2" plastic spreaders.
- Magnetic roller (for picking up screws on roof).

Large Equipment That Can Be Rented or Purchased
- Scissor lift.
- Auger (gas-powered post hole digger).
- Power washer.
- Floor blowers to dry wet carpet or tile.

Outside Tools
- Shovels: scoop, standard digging, and sharp shooter.
- Post hole digger.
- Steel rake, hoe.
- T-post pounder.
- Fertilizer spreader: can be used not only for fertilizer but also to spread ice melt on icy days.

Yard Work Tools (If You Are Responsible For Landscaping)
- 40" (at least) riding mower.
- Push mower for tight areas.
- Gas cans.
- Leaf blowers.
- String trimmer.
- Hedge trimmers.
- Limb trimmer.
- Chainsaw.
- Leaf rake.

Custodial Equipment
- Mop buckets, standard buckets.
- Mops, brooms, push brooms.

- Cleaning cart.
- Rags, sponges.
- Brushes.
- Dusting cloths, duster with extension for high areas.
- Toilet scrubbers.
- Toilet plungers.
- "Wet Floor" cones or signs.
- "Restroom Closed" signs (tension style that fits in frame of door).

Cleaning Chemicals

These may not be actual tools, but you need to have these on hand even if you have a janitorial service to do your main cleaning.

- Pine-Sol.
- Murphy's Oil Soap.
- PERdiem or universal cleaner for mopping floors, wiping countertops, etc.
- Super Sorb.
- Mr. Clean cleaning pads.
- Windex.
- Carpet cleaner and instant carpet spot cleaner.
- Bleach.
- Disinfectant spray.
- Disinfectant wipes.
- Goo Gone.
- CLR.
- Stainless steel cleaner.
- Odor absorber.
- Tile and stone cleaner.

CHAPTER 12
Technology

Truthfully, technology is my weak area, so this chapter will be very brief. Quite simply, I don't feel very qualified to cover this area, but I will list some of the programs I have used over my years in facilities and you can take it from there.

I joke with younger people that I've had a laptop since the '70s. I get a real strange look because most people know that personal computers didn't really show up until the early '80s, and laptops not until the '90s. I then explain that my first laptop was a yellow legal pad on my lap. (That is kind of a lame joke, isn't it?)

One other consideration is that, even if I were a software guru, everything I say here would be obsolete in six months to a year.

Anyway, the following list will give you an idea how technology is driving our field now. If you are starting out in facilities management, I'm confident you will do 90-plus percent of your work on cloud-based programs.

If your budget is limited, and you just need a simple way to list projects and inspections, you may look at the many free "lists" apps that are available.

There are software programs that will allow your staff to put in requests for repairs (lightbulbs, broken things, furniture repairs and assembling, etc.). Then, there is software to track all of your deficiencies, repairs, projects, inspections, and preventative maintenance.

There is software to schedule and reserve space for activities, and more software that will integrate your scheduling software to your HVAC system to schedule thermostat control.

Most programs also allow for tracking all of your assets (buildings, furniture, mechanical equipment, tools, etc.).

There are too many management software companies to list here, plus there will be half a dozen new ones in a month or two. So, here are a few programs you can research:

- Smartchurch.com (Espace)
- Facilio.com
- Upkeep.com
- Ramco.com
- eMaint CMMS
- Hippo CMMS
- FMX
- Asset Essentials
- Form.com
- Q Ware Facility Management
- mHelpDesk
- MaintMizer
- FTMaintenance
- Maintenance Connection
- Facilities Management eXpress
- Fiix
- MPulse
- Maintenance5000
- ManagerPlus
- MAPCON
- Agility by SSG Insight

CHAPTER 12: TECHNOLOGY

- Axxerion CMMS
- TabWare CMMS/EAM
- Maintenancecare.com

Then there are to-do list programs:

- Trello (I love this one)
- Todoist
- Toodledo
- Any.do
- Things
- TickTick
- Google Keep

There are document storage cloud sites:

- Google Drive (docs)
- Dropbox
- Box
- Apple iCloud
- Filecloud
- OneDriveforBusiness
- Egnyte
- Sharefile

If you need to design a project floor plan yourself for a committee or team to see your vision, these may help you:

- SmartDraw.com
- Room Sketcher
- Sketchup

- Sweethome3D
- AutoCAD LT
- Civil3D
- Draft it
- Floorplanner
- Roomie

As I have mentioned previously, there is now cloud-based software that will interface with many of your mechanical systems to allow you to have remote access to your building 24/7 from anywhere in the world using your laptop, tablet, or smart phone. This can include:

- Security and camera monitoring.
- Fire alarm monitoring.
- Access control (doors and/or exterior perimeter gates).
- Thermostat control.
- Lighting control.
- Utility usage monitoring (city or utility company).
- Landscape sprinkler system control.

Clerical software and hardware suggestions:
- MS Office Suite containing Word, Excel, Publisher.
- PDF converter.
- Desktop or phone app scanner.
- Multiple monitors to allow you to work on projects while still keeping camera views visible.

I'm not a doomsdayer (well, maybe a little), but in my opinion (and in court), it is necessary to keep hard copies of important documents, contracts, and other papers. It's a very

CHAPTER 12: TECHNOLOGY

good idea to keep notebooks with meeting or planning notes and white boards in your office to write ideas or to-do lists on and laminated calendars with reminders. This doesn't make you an "old fogey," but keeps you and your team accountable, and, as I noted earlier, when your boss walks by your office and sees all your projects and inspections in progress, well, that's always a good thing.

I can't believe I'm saying this, but technology is here to stay, so embrace it!

CHAPTER 13
Safety and Security Precautions

In Acts 20:7–12, we read about a young man named Eutychus. Bless his heart, he had a long day. His folks were both involved in the life of the church in Troas, and the Apostle Paul had been there for almost a week, and this was his last day before he was to leave. The members of the church had loved the time that Paul, the great missionary, had spent with them for the last several days. Now this last day was going to be a busy time of worship, teaching, food, and fellowship. It was truly an amazing day for this congregation of relatively new believers.

Eutychus was there all day for every service and teaching session, except, of course, when his mom probably sent him on errands to get something. He was worn out. He was excited as the sun started to set, thinking that things were about to wrap up, only to see the deacons of the church pulling out lamps and lighting them. For a teenager, that was not a good sign.

Well, this is a once-in-a-lifetime experience, he kept telling himself. That's what his mom had told him all week, because every night there had been teaching at members' homes, which everyone had been invited to. He knew this was a big deal, but he also knew he was very tired from a long day. As the teaching went on and on, Eutychus began to get sleepy and had a thought: *I'll sit in the window and the cool air from outside will keep me awake.*

So, about midnight, with Paul teaching away like a rock star, Eutychus climbed into a window and got comfortable. Well, he got *way* too comfortable.

Now, there's Paul; he was teaching with such power that even he was amazed at the presence of the Holy Spirit in the place. All of a sudden, someone screamed — and Eutychus's mother realized that her son had fallen from the window to the ground. Not just any fall either, but a fall from the third floor. Everyone ran down to check on the young man.

When Paul got downstairs, everyone was freaking out and crying and saying that Eutychus was dead. Paul worked his way through the crowd and leaned over the young man, gently picked his limp body up and leaned his ear close to the mouth and nose of Eutychus.

Paul looked up at everyone and said, "Do not be alarmed, for his life is in him."

They then carried the boy upstairs, worshipped by observing the Lord's Supper, and then they had an open share time. This is where it sure would be nice to know every detail of the night, but evidently after talking all night everyone got up and went home, including Eutychus and his family — and Paul, Silas, and Luke boarded a ship to go to another city to minister.

Now, I know that God performed a miracle here and raised Eutychus from the dead. We just don't know exactly the process of the healing. Did Paul's touch heal the young man? Whatever happened, it was a miracle from God that Eutychus lived, and we can give God alone the credit.

This was definitely an EAP (Emergency Action Plan) moment. Eutychus falling out of the window is the perfect example of why every church and organization needs an

CHAPTER 13: SAFETY AND SECURITY PRECAUTIONS

emergency action plan for accidents, whether it's a fall, heart attack, fire, or worse —something *will* happen. It's just about the last thing we plan for, and yet, when you put hundreds of people in a building, eventually something unplanned will happen. People get sick, unfortunately people drop over dead, people get hurt, smoke fills the building, bad storms take direct aim on the building, and the thing we hate to even mention, people who are not happy with life show up and make a scene either armed or unarmed.

The question I want to ask you is, are you ready to handle the worst of any of these situations if it arises?

The story of Eutychus should tell us more than anything about what we as church representatives and leaders should do in an emergency. Like Paul, we need to stay calm and keep everything going as "normal" as possible. When the temperature rises, we have to be thermostats, not thermometers.

The blessing for you as the facility guy is that you don't have to know everything. You just need to make sure that people have what they need in order to handle an emergency.

Emergency Action Plans

Yes, you should be CPR certified and know how to apply pressure on a wound, but hopefully you will not be the one who is administering first aid. For medical emergencies, you need to have church members who are medical professionals who can administer the medical expertise needed until the first responders arrive.

Let's start at the beginning. The very first thing that should happen to make any emergency a calmer experience is for two or three of the senior ministry staff to know that one of them must get on stage and calmly direct people and explain what they need to do. If you have a security team, they, along with the senior minister, will take the lead. They will decide if a medical emergency warrants evacuating the building or if someone can be moved to another location so the service can continue.

Back to your ministers – they should know how to evacuate people. There needs to be a plan for how to calmly get everyone out of the worship center without having a stampede. People should know where they go to pick up their children. If a weather emergency is coming, your ministers must know what interior rooms to direct people to, and they need to make it clear to people that their children are in a safe room in the other building and they will not be released until the weather event has passed.

Make sure there are posted evacuation maps and that your staff is properly trained in evacuating people from the building. As wonderful as it would be to have the congregation drill on how to evacuate, the best you can do in reality is to suggest to your pastors to take some time during a staff meeting and discuss and practice evacuation procedures.

If a dangerous situation arises with a possible violent person or people, like an active shooter, your security (safety) team or members who are in law enforcement will be responsible for making decisions on how to keep your people safe.

CHAPTER 13: SAFETY AND SECURITY PRECAUTIONS

Security Personnel: Paid and Volunteer

I do not by any means consider myself an expert on security. What I will share with you are some guidelines that I have seen followed. I will also suggest some things you should consider as you implement security measures in your church.

Before using any paid or volunteer security personnel, you need to run an in-house background check on them. It doesn't matter who they are or who they work for. You really should have your own paper trail and records for your security team's background checks.

Some states require that armed security personnel be actively employed by a state, county, or city law enforcement department that gives its officers permission to work as private security providers. Otherwise, your security people will not be able to carry handguns[4]. Make sure you know your state laws concerning armed private security before you proceed in hiring or training a security team.

Basically, your security team is that set of eyes that is always looking at people and who law-abiding people look to for peace of mind. This can be a big deterrent to crime all by itself. It stands to reason that if people planning to do harm in a social setting see security or people watching the property who look "official," they often leave or don't enter the property at all.

Whether you hire security or use volunteers, it is prudent

---

[4] Some states now allow volunteer safety team members to carry concealed weapons, as long as they are not in uniform and do not wear name tags that say security.

that you provide detailed parameters for them to operate under. They need to know what is expected of them and when it is expected. Your security team members should have it drilled into them that they are accountable and submissive to the church pastors and leadership as they provide security. They cannot go "Rambo" on just anyone or live out their secret desire to be a cop. They must be loving and humble servants as they boldly protect God's people.

Suggested List of Responsibilities For Security Team

- Walk around and check doors that should be locked and all areas of church.
- Be visible before services begin at the front entrance, lobby area, and the children's check-in area.
- Monitor and report to staff any unusual behavior (people wearing backpacks, bulky clothing, or carrying briefcases or packages, people wandering in parking lots or around building). Make it clear to security they are to contact a staff person if they see someone acting oddly who is not an imminent danger to anyone. There may be church members who have behavioral/social issues that might give off the wrong impression, but in reality they are no harm to anyone.
- Monitor cameras if equipment is available.
- Walk the parking lot at scheduled intervals checking for unusual activities or lights left on, etc.
- Sit in the worship center during services.
- Be qualified and prepared to administer first aid as needed.
- Be prepared to assist pastors/leadership in carrying

out emergency action plans (storm response, active shooter, theft, abuse response, crowd control, fire response, disturbance response, trespassing enforcement).

Determine When Security Is Required

- During worship services.
- Any time adults are meeting and childcare is provided (especially in a separate building).
- Any time a group over a certain number is in the building. Set a minimum number of people expected at an event for security to be provided, but 100 – 150 is a good starting place.
- During any type of 12-step recovery/addiction program.
- During church-wide events where the community is invited (picnics, VBS, fall events, etc.).

A good rule of thumb for in-house events (after hours meetings, training sessions, and the like) would be to lock the doors after the event begins so that no security is needed. A minister or volunteer may need to check the door periodically to assure no one running late is waiting to be let in.

How Much Security Do You Need?

Again, this will be determined by the location of your church, size of your church, time of day, and who is expected to attend the event.

If you have multiple buildings in use, you may need more

than one security person. You could choose to have one uniformed security person for parking lots and near the entrance to buildings, plus a plainclothes security person inside the building. You will always want a plainclothes security person to sit in services so as to not be a distraction.

Let's be perfectly honest here: your budget restrictions will be the main driver in determining how much security is provided at church events. If you can't pay for the proper security, then I would say it is better to use volunteer security (even if unarmed). The reasoning is because these people will have a real heart for taking care of people's safety. Also remember, regardless of budget constraints, you must have your volunteer security team background checked.

This is why, like I said earlier, it is important to know what members have a handgun concealed carry permit. These brothers and sisters in the Lord could be trained for the worst-case scenario.

It is imperative that you have a great relationship with local law enforcement. Like with contractors, it's a great idea to be on a first-name basis with the officers whose beat includes the church property and know the area captain or neighborhood safety officer. Establish a good rapport with them and also consult with them about how to handle emergency situations.

Once they arrive there to handle a security or emergency situation, in most cases they supersede any private security personnel you have. If you are not this point person, make sure a designated pastor or church leader assumes the role of point person for the church to establish this relationship.

Remember that security needs are usually based on something that has never happened to you and hopefully will

CHAPTER 13: SAFETY AND SECURITY PRECAUTIONS

never happen. When it comes to security, pray first for God's hand of protection over your people, then provide the best security you possibly can. You want your security people to feel as accepted and part of the team as any other staff member.

Provide the Following Resources For Your Security Team

- Phone numbers for you, pastor, associate pastor, children's minister, student minister.
- List of people (names and photos, if possible) who are under church discipline, have restraining orders against them, have no-trespass warnings against them, and any registered sex offenders, or cloud-based program or app that has a database of people with legal restrictions or record of dangerous behavior.
- First aid supplies.
- AED (defibrillator).
- Flashlights.
- Traffic cones.
- Car door unlocking tools.
- Booster cables or a booster system.
- Electronic tablet or smart phone to monitor cameras.
- Roll of yellow caution tape.
- A room for them to put their belongings and to occasionally relax (a good room for this would be where the camera monitors are located).
- Lanyards with proper identification for them to wear while on duty.
- Master key for them to use only when on duty, and a hex key to un-dog certain doors after events begin.

You need to show them any keys that are hidden for use on such things as door alarm reset devices, roof access hatches, storage rooms, etc.

Some churches have chosen to provide security a gun safe in a centralized locked room with biometric locks. There are additional handguns or rifles in it for use if the need arises. Only one church employee (who has handgun training and certification) and the security personnel should have access to this gun safe.

Additional Thoughts for Safety Procedures

Children's rooms should have a flip chart that outlines procedures for any given emergency. There should also be a flashlight in each children's room in case of power failure. If the children have to stay in their classroom in a lockdown situation, such as active shooter, there needs to be a way the room can be secured from the inside and children kept clear from view of windows in doors.

There needs to be a storm "safe" room or rooms in the children's area for all the kids. If bad weather (hurricane, tornado) is approaching, no one should be in an exterior room, and especially not in a room with windows. This room needs to have emergency lighting installed if possible, or LED lanterns kept in the room.

Earthquake protocols are also recommended where applicable. This would be as simple as designating open areas outside as safe zones and providing training for staff how to get under furniture (desks, heavy tables/counters) if they are unable to get outside in time.

CHAPTER 13: SAFETY AND SECURITY PRECAUTIONS

There needs to be an AED defibrillator in the children's building equipped with both child-sized and adult-sized pads. I would recommend keeping the AED near the check-in (front entrance) area.

There should also be a first aid kit in each building. A good place for first aid kits is in kitchen areas. Be sure to add quarterly inspection of first aid supplies to your inspection schedule. I recommend doing this at the same time you check the batteries in defibrillators.

There should be lockdown rooms in the adult areas as well. These are rooms that can protect people from bad weather or an active shooter situation. They should be on an inside hallway and able to be locked from the inside. If you have several rooms for adults, a staff person should be designated to be in each room.

You just can't be too careful. If bad weather is coming, someone should be watching the storm progress on a weather app and monitoring local weather advisories.

If a fire starts, there should be a way to know the building is completely evacuated. It's one thing to get people out of the building; it's a whole other task to get *everyone* out of the building. Ensure that prayer rooms and offices are empty. Sometimes when folks are in a private counseling or prayer time, they become oblivious to the world around them.

Make certain that if the children have to be evacuated that there is a dedicated place where they will be taken outside for their parents to pick them up. Good places would be playgrounds, basketball courts, or next to a garage or storage building. It needs to be somewhere obvious and safe. Also, please have an adequate number of baby beds equipped with large wheels for evacuation. This is the best way to evacuate children under two. Load those babies in a baby bed and roll them out.

Abuse Procedures and Precautions

This may be the most important thing you are responsible for in your ministry on a day of worship. Unfortunately, no one can be trusted.

- Your volunteers and team members need to be background-checked and have some child abuse prevention training.
- Volunteers are never to be alone with a child under 18 that is not their own child or in their guardianship.
- Volunteers are to report ANY inappropriate contact they see adult to child or child to child.
- Volunteers are to immediately report anyone who threatens to harm themselves or someone else.
- It's always okay to ask someone who looks out of place why they are in a certain area of the church. A simple "Can I help you find something?" is a good place to start.
- If a volunteer has not been background-checked, it should be explained to them that they cannot be left alone in the children's area until their background check clears.

There are people who will try to come in the children's building to see their children who may not be allowed that contact. These could be parents or relatives with restraining orders against them, or parents who do not have custody of

CHAPTER 13: SAFETY AND SECURITY PRECAUTIONS

their children who "just want to see their baby." Those with sex offender backgrounds should not be in the children's building at all and may very well have a distance limitation if they are on probation.

For this reason, areas not used in the children's building, and I would dare say all buildings, should be locked with the lights on during events. This keeps people out and allows you or others to see if someone is in there. All closets, custodial rooms, mechanical rooms, and storage rooms should be locked during any event.

All exterior doors that are not used as an entrance should be checked to make sure they are closed after an event gets started. People will sometimes prop doors open hoping to come back later and enter the building.

Have a camera system that can be monitored by security, and someone onsite should be trained on how to retrieve video from the DVR for police.

Make sure that anyone who has threatened another person in the church is accompanied by security at all times. Also, sometimes it is necessary to not allow that person on the premises. This may have to be enforced by a restraining order or a criminal trespass order. This sometimes requires a posted sign but usually only requires law enforcement or your security team to personally tell a person that, if they continue to come on the property, they will be arrested for trespassing on private property. It is good to limit the people that know this information. Lead pastors, of course, along with recovery/addiction counselors, and affected ministry leaders along with security team leaders constitute an example of those who need to know who these folks are.

Firearm Placard Posting and Handling Members Who Have Concealed Carry Permits

This section, like the rest of the book, is completely my opinion, and therefore not a legal document to be used in a court of law.

Unfortunately, in the time and culture we live, churches (and really any public area) have to be prepared for the possibility that someone may bring a firearm into the building to do harm or threaten someone. This can be tricky, especially in states that allow licensed concealed carry of firearms.

As hard as it can be to determine a policy on your property for firearms, your church leadership should make that decision and you need to post proper signage. Once you post signs, the church must then be ready to enforce a policy to ban all firearms or all except those who have a legal permit to concealed carry. Your organization may also choose to place no signage at entrances at all and handle each situation individually.

A word of caution here. Be careful before you completely ban all firearms from your facilities. If that is the direction your church chooses to go, then I hope you hire security that has access to firearms, or you have members who are in law enforcement who have permission from their employer and the church to carry weapons and act as security in the event an active shooter situation arises.

For example, in my state of Texas, it is legal to open carry a weapon, and it is legal to carry a concealed weapon if one has an LTC (license to carry) certification. The signage that covers Texas gun law is called the 30.06 and 30.07 Penal

CHAPTER 13: SAFETY AND SECURITY PRECAUTIONS

Code. The 30.06 sign bans LTC holders from carrying on the property. The 30.07 sign bans open carry of firearms on the property. Many churches choose only to post the 30.07 signage that bans open carry.

In most states, there are specific signs that must be posted at entrances to facilities that have the appropriate legal wording necessary to control carrying firearms on the property. In church we often desire to word posted signs with love and grace, but in this situation signage needs to be worded as required by the state.

Below are two websites that will help you in determining what signage you need in your facility. I would also recommend you check your state's official website to read the laws concerning restriction of firearms in public places:

- State by state requirements: www.gunstocarry.com/guns-laws-state/#states
- Signage specific to each state: www.safetysign.com/no-gun-signs-by-state

If your church allows licensed concealed carry holders to enter the property with their weapons, I would recommend that you or your pastor try to determine who has an LTC in your congregation, then let the security team leader know this. You, a minister, or the security team leader may then need to contact each of these people to talk with them about how they are expected to react if an active shooter situation arises, and emphasize that the security team will always take the lead and direct them what to do with their firearm in the event of an emergency.

Preparing For Annual Fire Inspection

Verify the following items are in order prior to the annual fire inspection:

- Fire extinguisher inspection is current.
- Fire alarm inspection is current.
- Fire suppression system inspection is current.
- Knox box has proper items in it (master key, security system code, and your phone number). This can only be done when the fire department is present as they are the only ones with a key.
- Exit sign lights and emergency lights work.
- Exits clear and accessible.
- Aisles in worship center wide enough for safe evacuation (check local fire codes).
- No paint stored inside the buildings (some cities allow paint storage inside).
- No flammable items next to water heater or in air handler rooms.
- Fire alarm pull stations properly set and not obstructed.
- Portable heaters and large appliances are plugged directly into the wall outlet (I also recommend that no residential style extension cords be used anywhere).
- Check all GFCI outlets for proper operation.

Be Aware of ADA (Americans with Disabilities Act) Requirements

As you remodel or build new buildings, be aware of the laws and restrictions for ADA. This could really be tricky if you

CHAPTER 13: SAFETY AND SECURITY PRECAUTIONS

have an older building. I would recommend that in older buildings you go ahead and change the doorknobs to lever-style in public areas, install handicap bars in restrooms, have paper towel dispensers low enough for someone in a wheelchair to reach, and install faucets with lever-style handles. Also, make sure there are designated areas for wheelchairs in the worship center and large classrooms.

These kinds of changes aren't huge expenditures and will demonstrate to handicapped people that even though the building may not be completely ADA-compliant because of its age, the church does care about them being able to function in the building as best as they can.

Many older buildings are often "grandfathered in" when the Certificate of Occupancy (CO) is renewed and do not have to be ADA-compliant. Below are three things to be sensitive of that could cost you a lot of money:

- If a large amount of work is done to the building (usually over $50,000), sometimes the city or state will require everything be brought up to ADA minimums.
- If a new building is constructed that physically touches the old building, you probably will be required to bring ADA up to current code in the older building that matches the new building.
- If there are major changes made to the main entrance of a building, the city may require that everything associated with that entrance also be brought up to current ADA requirements, like ramps, automatic door openers, signage, etc.

JAMES D. JORDAN

Dealing With Infectious Diseases

While writing this book, the worldwide 2020 pandemic caused by COVID-19 was in full swing.

In the middle of March 2020, the federal government, most state governors, and local governments basically shut down the US for several months, including churches. It was quite a process.

In my state, we were told that no more than 500 could meet together, then it became no more than 250, then no more than fifty, then houses of worship were asked along with other non-essential businesses and organizations not to be open at all. Later, groups of ten or more were asked not to meet anywhere, which basically knocked out most Sunday School classes and home groups from meeting offsite

So, there we were. No one was at our campuses "officially," but the facilities team had been designated as essential personnel, so they were there to sanitize everything, repair everything, and work on projects (which is about the only bright side to such a situation).

Again, during a pandemic or other national emergency, your state and local authorities will set standards and limitations of how many can come in your buildings. As I earlier stated, your facilities team may or may not be considered essential personnel. Your pastor and staff will need counsel from you here in making a determination whether and how often your folks need to be onsite, and what is expected from them as far as interaction with church members who come to the church facility. Make sure that your supervisor/minister knows that you will not put yourself or your people at risk. In such hard times, the safety of your

CHAPTER 13: SAFETY AND SECURITY PRECAUTIONS

team should never be too far from your mind.

Now, as I've reminded other facility managers, it's not your decision about building use and policies during this time. You might be asked about your thoughts on it, but if I were you, let the pastors and elders in your church make and enforce the decisions about who has access to buildings. This will take a heap of pressure off of you.

As a facilities department, here is what you can do during high-risk infectious disease events:

1. Make sure all hard surfaces get sanitized on a regular basis:
    a. Exterior doors (metal hardware).
    b. Interior door hardware (doorknobs).
    c. Countertops and water fountains.
    d. Restroom fixtures and kitchen areas.
    e. Hard-surface floors mopped regularly.
    f. Hard-surface chairs and tables in classrooms, children areas, etc.
2. Keep a good supply of disinfectant cleaners, like Lysol, Murphy's oil soap, and others for disinfecting and cleaning.
3. Keep a good supply of paper goods, soap, and hand sanitizer for restrooms and hallway dispensers.
4. Have a setup plan for remote ministry rooms specifically for high-risk individuals (worship center, classrooms, fellowship hall, etc.).
5. Purchase several handheld number clickers in case your city only allows a certain number of people in the

buildings. Radios may also be needed if you have several entrances.

6. Have social distance stickers, stanchions, or cones available to keep folks going in the safest direction.

7. You may be asked to purchase digital infrared thermometers if needed for screening people as well. Sorry, I had to mention this, as impersonal as it sounds.

8. Require that all package, postal, and supply deliveries be made at a specific location or entrance.

9. Make sure to provide your team, custodians, and possibly even contractors with the necessary PPE to insure the safety of all.

10. Be ready to mix up home recipes of cleaning solution, in case supplies and suppliers have distribution issues or delivery delays. There are several bleach-based recipes for cleaning solution that you can find on the internet. If you prefer to use non-toxic ingredients, you can also find vinegar-based recipes for cleaning.

11. I also recommend that you keep several extra spray bottles, a pump-up backpack sprayer, and a hydrostatic sprayer to use for disinfecting areas as needed.

12. Consider installing air purification technology to your HVAC system. Here are some systems I am aware of:
    a. HEPA
    b. Activated carbon
    c. UV-C (ultraviolet light)
    d. Negative ion (bipolar ionization)
    e. Ozone

CHAPTER 13: SAFETY AND SECURITY PRECAUTIONS

    f.   Heat recovery/energy recovery (HRV/ERV)

Portable air purifiers can also be purchased that use most of the above technology. Of course, using high MERV (11-14) filters, following good cleaning and disinfecting procedures, and turning on HVAC well in advance of events is a good way to economically keeping your buildings as safe and healthy as possible.

We have never seen anything like the 2020 pandemic that has so upended the way we think about corporate gatherings. I have a feeling *social distancing* will be in our vocabulary from now on. But please remember this foremost: the church is meant to be serving, enjoying fellowship, encouraging, ministering, and worshiping together.

"And let us not neglect our meeting together, as some people do, but encourage one another, especially now that the day of his return is drawing near." —Hebrews 10:25 (NLT)

Whenever these shutdowns or other emergencies happen, be careful, be prepared, and also be ready for that glorious day when the church will come back together for the glory of God!

Chapter 14
Budgets That Make Sense and Get Things Done

Your budget prep for the following year could be one of the most productive things you do the whole year. Budget planning is not hard, but it is time-consuming and must be specific. One fatal flaw of budget planning is leaving off something really important. That's why it's always best to use the current year's budget as your template for the next year's budget.

As you plan a budget, think about what you need for a line item. One line item may only need funding once a year, while another line item may be quarterly. There will be many line items that will be used every month. There are things you might fight for in your budget, then not do. It's always better to have it than not.

Another good tool for budget planning is to get a copy of your facility budget reports and variance reports for a period of twelve full months. If you use a January – December budget year, you may want to get June – May of the previous year's records so you will have a full twelve-month cycle to use in your budget planning.

What we are going to do is just go through a budget, and I'll list what the needs may be as far as interval of need. I will not list amounts because those costs will be different for every facility. Here are most of the topics in a budget and what items fall in them:

- **Administration:** Covers your office supplies, organizational membership fees like IFMA and NACFM, and conference fees (professional development). For the most part, this will be money set aside only in certain months.
- **Supplies:** Includes cleaning supplies, paper goods, water machine filters, coffee supplies. This could be every month, or four times a year for some items.
- **Custodial Contractors:** Includes contracted custodian service and contracted day porter (setup helper). This will be a monthly expense.
- **Utilities:** Electrical, water, gas, trash pickup, internet service, or streaming service. These will also be monthly expenses.
- **Repairs and In-house Maintenance:** These are funds used to cover sporadic or one-time maintenance needs. For example, hiring a carpenter and painter if a wall gets damaged, having a fence repaired, or hanging new shelves or cabinets in an existing space.
- **Maintenance:** Includes repairs for electrical, plumbing, HVAC, and basically any other unscheduled repair like broken windows, door repairs, carpet repairs, etc.
- **Preventative Maintenance:** Used for scheduled inspections and maintenance such as HVAC quarterly inspections, fire extinguisher inspections, hood inspection.
- **Inspections and Permits:** Covers state and city-required inspections and permits, including fire alarm inspection, annual fire inspection, fire alarm permit, backflow inspections, and elevator inspections.

CHAPTER 14: BUDGETS THAT MAKE SENSE AND GET THINGS DONE

- **Monitoring:** Monthly fees you pay to the monitoring company for fire alarm and security system.
- **Rentals:** Covers items like renting a U-Haul, tools, lifts.
- **Signage:** Sign repair or interior door placard changes.
- **Special Projects:** Your wish list for projects you or the staff want to do. It may also include new HVAC units or major tools.
- **Security Personnel:** Contracted fees you pay your security personnel on days of worship.

Now let's look at all this in a more visually friendly format:

Facilities Budget Template Example		
Budget Topic	Item Description	Frequency of Invoicing
City Fees	Annual fire inspection	Annually
City Fees	Alarm permit fee	Annually
Fees	Fire alarm monitoring	Monthly
Fees	Security alarm monitoring	Monthly
Fees & Inspection	Backflow testing	Annually
Fees & Inspection	Fire extinguisher inspection	Annually
Fees & Inspection	Kitchen ansul (exhaust hood) inspection	Semi-annually

Facilities Budget Template Example		
Fees & Inspection	Fire alarm inspection and repairs	Annually
Fees & Inspection	Vehicle and trailer registration and inspection	Annually
Fees & Inspection	Elevator inspection and repair	Annually
Fees & Inspection	Fire sprinkler inspection and repairs	Annually
Utilities	Water	Monthly
Utilities	Electric	Monthly
Utilities	Natural gas	Monthly
Utilities	Trash and recycling pickup	Monthly or Weekly
Utilities	Internet and cloud server service	Monthly
Utilities	Remote access software subscriptions	Monthly
Utilities	Property and vehicle insurance	Semi-annually or Monthly

CHAPTER 14: BUDGETS THAT MAKE SENSE AND GET THINGS DONE

Facilities Budget Template Example

Utilities	CMMS subscription (facility management software)	Annually or Monthly
Ministry Expenses	NACFM membership (association membership)	Annually
Ministry Expenses	IFMA membership (association membership)	Annually
Ministry Expenses	General office supplies	Semi-annually
Ministry Expenses	Meal for hosting NACFM events	Annually
Ministry Expenses	Uniforms	Semi-annually
Ministry Expenses	Volunteer appreciation meal	Annually
Ministry Expenses	Business cards	Annually
Ministry Expenses	Business expenses- (mileage/meals)	Monthly
Ministry Expenses	Professional development (courses or conferences)	Annually

Facilities Budget Template Example		
Fixed Pricing Contracts	Security officers	Monthly
Fixed Pricing Contracts	Day porter or facilities associates	Bi-weekly
Fixed Pricing Contracts	Janitorial service	Monthly
Fixed Pricing Contracts	Landscaping (mowing)	Monthly
Fixed Pricing Contracts	Field mowing (with tractor)	Quarterly (or as needed)
Fixed Pricing Contracts	First aid supplies	Quarterly
Fixed Pricing Contracts	Pest control	Quarterly
Fixed Pricing Contracts	HVAC preventative maintenance	Quarterly or semi-annually
Fixed Pricing Contracts	Water dispenser maintenance	Semi-annually
Supplies	Cleaning supplies	Monthly (as needed)
Supplies	Restroom/paper supplies	Monthly (as needed)
Supplies	Kitchen supplies	Monthly (as needed)
Supplies	Hardware for in-house projects	Monthly (as needed)

CHAPTER 14: BUDGETS THAT MAKE SENSE AND GET THINGS DONE

Facilities Budget Template Example		
Supplies	Signage (replacement and repair)	As needed
Supplies	Special project supplies	As needed
Supplies	Tool purchases	Semi-annually
Supplies	Keys and key fobs	Annually
Supplies	Light bulb replacement and fixture repair	Monthly (as needed)
Supplies	Office furniture	As needed
Supplies	Lobby furniture	As needed
Supplies	Folding tables & chairs	As needed
Repairs & Maintenance	Electrical repairs	As needed
Repairs & Maintenance	Plumbing repairs	As needed
Repairs & Maintenance	HVAC repairs	As needed
Repairs & Maintenance	Roof repairs	As needed
Repairs & Maintenance	Miscellaneous repairs	As needed
Repairs & Maintenance	Parking lot maintenance	Annually or as needed

Facilities Budget Template Example		
Repairs & Maintenance	Irrigation sprinkler repairs	As needed
Repairs & Maintenance	Door repair	As needed
Repairs & Maintenance	Elevator repairs	As needed
Repairs & Maintenance	Gym floor buffing	Quarterly
Repairs & Maintenance	Grease trap cleaning	Annually
Repairs & Maintenance	Tool rental	As needed
Repairs & Maintenance	U-Haul rental	As needed
Repairs & Maintenance	Lift rental	As needed (semi-annually)
Repairs & Maintenance	Porta-Potty rental	As needed
Communication	New signs and seasonal signage	As needed
Communication	EAP print materials	Annually
Communication	Parent safety brochures	Annually
Special Request Projects	Item	Requested by
Request	Reseal and restripe parking lots	Facilities request

CHAPTER 14: BUDGETS THAT MAKE SENSE AND GET THINGS DONE

Facilities Budget Template Example		
Request	Paint building exterior	Facilities request
Request	New carpet in offices	Staff request
Request	Reconfigure lobby	Lead pastor
Request	New carpet extractor	Facilities request

The budget items above are applicable to your property and ministry and flexible however you need to set it up. For instance, the office supplies, ministry expenses, business expenses, professional development, business cards, and uniforms may need to come out of the administration, personnel, or HR budgets of the church's general budget rather than your specific budget.

As you work on your budget, *prayer is a priority*, *vision is vital* (DREAM!), but *realism is required* (you must understand what your church can afford). If your parking lot looks terrible, get some bids and put it in your requested projects. If all your HVAC is brand new, you may be able to lower monthly repairs almost to zero for a few years.

Remember to have a clear justification for your requests. If you cannot explain why you need something, maybe you don't need it. Special project requests for ministry purposes should always have a minister's support.

For your monthly repairs and hardware needs, add a little more than what you think you will use. This "cushion" in your budget will help you be able to do some of those last-minute projects or minor repairs that jump up and surprise you when you least expect it. Your finance team will be thrilled you don't have to run to them every month to ask for a few hundred dollars to fix a water fountain or broken window.

Budgets sound scary, but, in reality, they are the thing that can really empower you on a day-to-day basis by not enslaving you and will truly free you to be responsible and creative with the gifts God's people have brought into His storehouse (Malachi 3:8 – 10).

Which brings up another good point about your ability to spend money: there needs to be a clear understanding how you spend your budget. I would suggest a $3,000 – $5,000 limit on what you can spend without going to your boss or committee, and another understanding that, especially during the warm months, HVAC repairs are a priority and have to be taken care of ASAP. One thing that would help with accountability for you would be to have one or two people you could at least email to inform of a major repair which is needed before service time that you need to move on immediately.

Another thing to remember is every church goes through financial difficulties. Please be sensitive to these lean times. One of the best things you could do is to have an emergency budget tucked in your back pocket (so to speak) that you can implement if things get tight. This emergency budget would be a bare bones budget to take care of required inspections, permits, security, preventative maintenance that is under contract, utilities, insurance, basic paper and cleaning supplies, minimal janitorial service, and major repairs that cannot be put off. These are the times you can really lean on your volunteers to help you with minor to medium repairs, which can end up saving the church thousands of dollars.

God has given you an amazing responsibility to take care

CHAPTER 14: BUDGETS THAT MAKE SENSE AND GET THINGS DONE

of His house. Take your budget and be the steward of that budget the way God wants. If your church budget is tight, then pray for God's people to give, and if God has blessed your church financially, be thankful and consider the blessing of a good budget and the opportunity to show how excellent your God is in His buildings.

CHAPTER 15
Network With Other Facility Managers

This is my get-in-your-face moment. I know you are busy. I know you have a page full of projects looking at you every day, and they won't go away. Guess what: if you had ten full-time people on your staff, thirty volunteers, and a million-dollar budget, you would still have a wall full of projects and be as nervous as a long-tailed cat in a room full of rocking chairs about leaving your property during the work day.

I was talking to a facility manager one day and encouraging him to attend a local CFM meeting, and he told me he is just too busy most days to break away for 2 – 3 hours. What's funny is that, a few minutes before, I overheard him telling someone how great his number two guy was and how he trusted him to do anything when he is not around.

The bottom line is that we all need a couple of hours away once a month or so to meet with people who are dealing with the same issues we deal with. You need people like you to network with.

There are at least three organizations you can join nationally:

1. **The IFMA (International Facility Managers Association)** is a secular organization that has a national membership, and, in many larger metro areas, they have an active local chapter. Yes, you have to join, but many local chapters meet monthly or quarterly and tour buildings and share a

meal together.

2. **WFX – Worship Facilities Expo** is an expo-type organization that specializes in hosting trade shows with training for administrators, facility managers, and techies.

3. The best choice, in my opinion, for church facility managers is to join the **NACFM (National Association of Church Facility Managers)**. There is a national membership fee, but many of the local chapters welcome non-members to attend their monthly meetings. This is a great group of ladies and men who share ideas and contacts, hear vendor presentations on new products, eat really good food, and have great fellowship. NACFM also has a certification program that will allow you to attain a nationally-recognized certification. During the training program for the certification you will meet people who will become lifelong friends. The annual NACFM conference is held at different locations around the country and offers a great time of worship, teaching, seminars, fellowship, and encouragement for you and your spouse as well.

You may also want to connect with facility managers in your local denomination or associations and have fellowship with them. In this way, you can have an "informal" way to network and share ideas, especially if you are not near enough to a metropolitan area to conveniently attend one of the larger gatherings mentioned above.

Yes, you will feel guilty when you leave your church to attend one of these meetings, but you will be glad you went. Even when you don't need the information presented, the

CHAPTER 15: NETWORK WITH OTHER FACILITY MANAGERS

fellowship and encouragement will be awesome. You will be grateful to connect with these people, even if you only attend randomly. I promise you this, your buildings will be there when you get back, waiting on you to be a better facility manager because you learned something, found a new resource, or simply released a little stress through great fellowship.

Chapter 16
Now Let's Start Managing Your Facilities

Wow, I can't believe this is the last chapter. As I said early on, I know I have not covered every detail of church facility management, and a lot of you who are smarter than me maybe could have explained stuff a lot better. What I hope I was able to convey is how amazing this ministry is to the church and how you get a 50-yard-line seat to see God do incredible things in people's lives through His buildings.

I want to finish this book with some thoughts about character. In the movie *Life With Father*, the father is asked by a maid service manager about the character of the house, and his classic answer is, "Madam, *I* am the character of my house." Okay, it's much funnier on film...

Men and ladies reading this, if you don't remember anything else from this book, please remember this: your character as a facility manager is everything. You might call something by the wrong name, or forget to have an inspection done on time, but your godly character is what will touch people's lives. That is what will last.

When it comes to work ethic in today's world, I love a quote from Tom Brokaw's book *The Greatest Generation* that states:

"This generation was united not only by a common purpose, but also by common values – duty, honor, economy, courage, service, love of family and country, and, above all,

responsibility for oneself."[5]

As much as I like this list, to be true to this book's theme I have one more list to share with you. Big surprise, huh?

Be a Good Spouse and Parent

Your first priority, after loving Jesus, is to love your family well. Love your spouse, put her or him on a pedestal, and give them the time they deserve. Yes, they will be home a lot when you are at the church on days of worship, Wednesday nights, and when fire and security alarms go off at 3:00 a.m. It took me a long time to get this part down, but please take time to be with them. If they need you, go. If your kids need you, go.

Like I said in the last chapter, the buildings won't go anywhere, and I promise there are people in your church who will love to cover for you. Sure, they may not have a clue what to do, but if they can lock doors, turn off lights, and have your phone number, everything will be fine.

I mentioned it before, but the second greatest command in Matthew 22:39b says, "You shall love your neighbor as yourself" (ESV). Let me give you a little free advice here: your number one neighbor is your spouse and then your family.

Be Yourself

A lot of us wish we could talk or write or sing like some-

---

[5] Brokaw, Tom. *Greatest Generation, The* (New York: Random House, Inc. 1998) from book flap.

CHAPTER 16: NOW LET'S START MANAGING YOUR FACILITIES

one else. Well, God made you like you are for a reason, and He didn't do that for you to wish you could be someone else. He gave you the personality you have. You may be shy, or not able to talk well in front of people, or maybe you just feel awkward around people, yet you love to serve and use your hands.

I will repeat myself: He called *you* to be a church facility manager, right? Then don't worry. Be who God made you to be, and people will love you.

Be On Time

A lot of people joke that they are fashionably late to a meeting. Everyone laughs, then things get going. Guess what? No one is really laughing inside. What your boss or pastor wants and respects is people who are early to a meeting or an event and folks who have their things set up and ready to go beforehand.

Being on time doesn't require a 4.0 grade point average, wearing nice clothes, or having a degree on your office wall. Quite simply, being on time just requires the responsibility to "be on time," and it might just help your career flourish as much as anything else you do at work.

Be Flexible

Learn how to play well with others. Listen, and even go along with others' ideas. You are the facility manager, you control one of the largest budgets in the church, but I will promise you that at some point in your career your pastor is going to look you in the eyes and tell you to build that accent wall the way the 25-year-old children's minister wants to unless it is unsafe or way too expensive.

Now this example may be a little extreme, but I hope you will understand that, by being flexible and understanding of others' ideas, you will create trust and confidence of others in your work and your ideas. And, if that accent wall in the children's area doesn't work, and it needs to be redone *your* way? Well, then I call that "job security."

Also, here's a little fact we need to put to bed. Facility managers have a reputation in the secular world of being difficult and inflexible. So, why don't we change that perception and let God show people what His love looks like in facilities management?

Be Honest

What else can I say? We live in a world where it's almost accepted to tell "little white lies" about your progress on a project. So many people think that no one will know if they say they did something, even if it isn't quite done yet. Hey, just say you still need to finish it. It just isn't worth it to bend the truth, even a little. So, that's it. Be honest all the time, even if it gets you a little slap on the hand.

Pray, Pray, Then Pray Some More

Everything you do should be bathed in prayer. Every project, every relationship, every difficult conversation, and every blessing. Don't stop praying.

CHAPTER 16: NOW LET'S START MANAGING YOUR FACILITIES

Give God the Glory

After leading worship for thirty years, I wasn't sure what it would be like to be a behind-the-scenes person as a facility manager, and honestly, there was a little adjustment for me. I loved leading worship, but God was calling me to something else. Little did I know God was getting ready to do something huge for Susan and me.

Over the next few years as a facility manager, I felt God's presence in my life and His hand on my life as much or more as when I led worship. God did something in my life that to this day I really can't explain. All I know is He was at work laying things out for my facility manager career years before I ever did it for a paycheck. I'm almost in tears as I think of what God has done for me.

He can and will do the same for you. You have been hired to be a church facility manager, but really you have been called by the Master Facility Manager to take care of His house, to make it a safe harbor for the hurting heart, and a place for believers to worship and encourage others.

Closing Thought

I am sure there are terms, topics, and technologies that I have failed to address or that have come up since the printing of this book. You should be able to find a website, blog, newsletter, or contractor to keep you current on the latest trends.

My prayer and hope for you is that facility management will not be a burden or a task that you dread doing, but that every day you go to work you will seek diligently for God to show up in everything you do and give you opportunities to show His love to everyone you encounter.

Now, with a grateful heart for each of you called to the facilities ministry, I leave you with these words from 1 Corinthians 1:4-9 (ESV), "I give thanks to my God always for you because of the grace of God that was given you in Christ Jesus, that in every way you were enriched in Him in all speech and all knowledge – even as the testimony about Christ was confirmed among you – so that you are not lacking in any gift, as you wait for the revealing of our Lord Jesus Christ, who will sustain you to the end, guiltless in the day of our Lord Jesus Christ. God is faithful, by whom you were called into the fellowship of his Son, Jesus Christ our Lord."

And by the way, while you are creating a safe harbor for people to worship in, will you move that new wall over three more feet, please?

Give God the glory!

REFERENCE SECTION

Scripture References

Chapter 1
Story of Bezalel, from Exodus 31
Story of Zerubbabel, from Ezra and Nehemiah

Chapter 2
Work in Progress, Philippians 2:12

Chapter 3
Healing of Paralytic, Mark 2:1-12 and Luke 5:17-21

Chapter 4
Creation, Genesis 1-2
Building the Ark, Genesis 6
The Ten Commandments, Exodus 20
Principles of the Good Shepherd, Psalm 23
Six, No Seven Things That God Hates, Proverbs 6:16-19
The Godly Woman, Proverbs 31:10-31
The Genealogy of Jesus Christ, Matthew 1:1-17
The Beatitudes, Matthew 5
The Spiritual Gifts, Romans 12 and 1 Corinthians 12
The Fruits of the Spirit, Galatians 5

Chapter 5
Second Greatest Commandment, Matthew 22:39
God's Thoughts, Isaiah 55:8
God's Ways, Psalm 25:4-5

Chapter 6
Serving, Mark 10:45
Foot Washing, John 13

Chapter 7
Building the Tabernacle, Exodus 25:8
Wages of Hired Worker, Leviticus 19:13

Chapter 13
Story of Eutychus, from Acts 20:7-12
Meeting Together, Hebrews 10:25

Chapter 14
Bringing Tithes Into the Storehouse, Malachi 3:8-10

Chapter 16
Second Greatest Commandment, Matthew 22:39
Paul's Thanksgiving Prayer, 1 Corinthians 1:4-9

Book References

Chapter 7
P. Andreas. *Construction Project Management Success, The, Third Edition.* (Lexington: Self-Published, 2015) pg. 36

Gould, Fred. *Construction Project Management, Third Edition* (Upper Saddle River: Pearson-Prentice Hall, 2008) pg. 7

Portny, Stanley E. *Project Management for Dummies* (Hoboken: John Wiley & Sons, Inc. 2013) pg. 265

Chapter 16
Brokaw, Tom. *Greatest Generation, The* (New York: Random House, Inc. 1998) from book flap.

ABOUT THE AUTHOR

James has been married to Susan for over thirty-seven years, and they have four children and seven grandchildren. He served as a minister of music for nearly thirty years in various churches in Texas before the Lord called him to the facilities ministry.

He served as a crew chief on fighter jets in the U.S. Air Force from 1975 – 1979 and received his Bachelor's degree with an emphasis in pastoral ministries from Dallas Baptist University in 1990. He has managed many construction and remodeling projects for the churches he has served as well as doing the day-to-day functions of a facility manager since 2012. In 2016, he became a Certified Church Facility Manager with the NACFM. In 2019, he retired from full-time ministry but continues to help churches as a facility consultant.

James continues to have a heart for facilities as he guides facility managers and pastors in the importance of keeping church facilities in a condition that truly honors our Lord.

Made in United States
Orlando, FL
10 December 2022

25973633R00143